A Treatise On Milch Cows

Francis Guenon

In the interest of creating a more extensive selection of rare historical book reprints, we have chosen to reproduce this title even though it may possibly have occasional imperfections such as missing and blurred pages, missing text, poor pictures, markings, dark backgrounds and other reproduction issues beyond our control. Because this work is culturally important, we have made it available as a part of our commitment to protecting, preserving and promoting the world's literature. Thank you for your understanding.

A

TREATISE

ON

MILCH COWS,

WHEREBY

THE QUALITY AND QUANTITY OF MILK

WHICH ANY COW WILL GIVE MAY BE ACCURATELY DETERMINED BY OBSERVING NATURAL MARKS OR EXTERNAL INDICATIONS ALONE; THE LENGTH OF TIME SHE WILL CONTINUE TO GIVE MILK, &c.

By M. FRANCIS GUENON,
OF LIBOURNE, FRANCE.

TRANSLATED FOR THE FARMERS' LIBRARY, FROM THE FRENCH,
By N. P. TRIST, ESQ.
LATE UNITED STATES CONSUL AT HAVANA.

WITH INTRODUCTORY

REMARKS AND OBSERVATIONS,

ON THE

COW AND THE DAIRY.

By JOHN S. SKINNER,

Forty-fifth Thousand—With Additions.

NEW YORK:
T. L. McELRATH AND COMPANY,
17 SPRUCE STREET.
1854.

Entered, according to Act of Congress, in the year 1846,
BY GREELEY & McELRATH,
in the Clerk's Office of the District Court of the United States, in and for the Southern District of New York.

FOURTEENTH EDITION.

NATIONAL TRIBUTE OF THE FRENCH GOVERNMENT

TO

M. GUENON,

FOR HIS VALUABLE DISCOVERY WITH REGARD TO

MILCH COWS.

PENSION OF THREE THOUSAND FRANCS A YEAR TO THE AUTHOR.

Paris, *Sept.* 17, 1848.

Messrs. Greeley & McElrath:

The National Assembly's *Committee on Agriculture* have unanimously voted to confer on M. Guenon a pension of *three thousand francs* a year, in consideration of his discovery of an infallible method for determining the capacities of milch cows. This method is the same as has become so generally known and appreciated throughout the United States, through the medium of that excellent little work published by you containing a translation of M. Guenon's treatise on the subject.

The committee, in the report (which will soon be presented to the Assembly, and no doubt adopted with unanimity), say that the method has been subjected to the most thorough tests, and that no doubt can exist as to its infallibility ; by following the directions of M. Guenon, as laid down in the treatise, any one can tell with certainty whether a cow is a good milker, or whether a young heifer will become one, so that there need be no doubt as to the profit of raising an animal, and no chance of being taken in in the purchase of one. By this means the farmer may select among his young calves those that will give abundance of milk when they are raised, and dispose of the rest at once for the shambles. No breeder of cattle need be told of the immense advantages which such a guide confers.

The committee say that a discovery of this nature, which adds so largely to the actual worth of the country, is pre-eminently deserving of a national acknowledgment, and they accordingly propose that the Republic confer upon M. Guenon the pension of three thousand francs as a testimony of the estimation in which it holds his services as a public benefactor.

Against such an appropriation of the public money there can be no objection. How much more rational it is that pensions and honors should be bestowed upon those who, by valuable scientific discoveries, by improvements in agriculture and manufactures, render themselves permanently useful to the world, than upon cheating politicians and successful soldiers.

Yours respectfully, C. A. D.

REPORT TO THE NATIONAL ASSEMBLY.

The congress had just expressed a wish that "*Guenon's Theory of the Milk-giving Properties of Cows*," published some years since, should be thoroughly examined and reported on when M. Guenon himself arrived in Paris. Called here on business of a private nature, he readily set aside everything to place himself at the disposal of your honorable body.

After many disappointments, he came to ask of you a public expression of your approbation, and of the country, an exhibition of national gratitude for a discovery surrendered without reserve to the common good, when he might have kept his secret to himself, with its certain emoluments.

A just love of celebrity, perhaps even the vague hope of a recompense proportioned to the service he had rendered the country, brought him to your bar, and placed him under your patronage.

It was immediately decided that a committee should accompany him to some dairy, and there apply and demonstrate the principles he has promulgated. If a decisive test confirmed all that you were led to expect, it became you, gentlemen, to give from this spot — the great centre of knowledge — a striking consecration, too long desired, of Mr. Guenon's singular discovery.

The farmer exercises an art essentially practical, and will not reject an obviously useful process because he may not appear to understand it. His science is that of facts, which he studies with a view to their application.

In obedience to your call, forty or fifty members of the congress assembled on the 30th of March, to enter upon the investigation that you had ordered. At the head of your committee were two of your presidents — M. Fouquier d'Herroul, known for his eminent services as chairman of the committee on cattle, and M. Dupin, who is always to be found at his post where the national interest is concerned. Other distinguished agriculturists were upon the committee, and the intelligent and ingenious man on whose account this meeting was held, and for whom the investigation was to be decisive, accompanied it, with a calm confidence derived from the hope of an impartial decision and a deep conviction of his rights.

Arrived at the dairy, thirteen cows were offered for inspection :—

2 Cotentines,* thorough-bred.
1 Cotentine, half-blood.
6 Normans, more or less crossed.
1 Swiss.
3 of Flemish and Durham blood.

Before proceeding to the proof, Mr. Guenon called our attention to the fact that the exceptional manner in which the Parisian cows were fed, might produce some abnormal results. This was considered a sufficient reason to allow a latitude of one or two pints to his estimate, instead of anticipating the exact results which he claims under ordinary circumstances.

As soon as a cow was brought out, the amount of milk which she gave for two or three weeks after calving, was privately made known to the committee, and immediately put down in writing. Mr. Guenon was then called upon to examine the revealing signs, and without being allowed to touch the cow, gave his estimate, which was likewise set down. The amount of milk furnished by the cows submitted for examination, varied from fourteen to twenty-four pints.

In eleven of the cases, the estimate of Guenon proved to be correct, and there was some uncertainty about another cow recently purchased, that had been sick since she was bought.

* So called from Cotentin, a district of country from lower Normandy.

Finally, upon the Anglo-Flemish cow there appeared a notable difference between the rather precipitate estimate of Mr. Guenon, who calculated her yield at fifteen pints, and her known yield, which was twenty-two pints; but this mistake had been corrected beforehand, by one of our most intelligent colleagues — M. Collot — who has been applying Mr. Guenon's theory for several years past, and who had at first sight estimated the yield of the Anglo-Flemish cow at twenty pints, a near approximation to the truth. So that we may say in this case, that Mr. Guenon, and not his method, was at fault.

On most of the animals inspected, Mr. Guenon pointed out to the audience the revealing signs upon which his system is founded, and referring to the printed treatise before us, showed the relation of the principle to the results. He took care only (in view of the excess of feed given to cows in the Paris dairy) to add a certain amount to the normal valuation given in his book; for the treatise of Mr. Guenon supposes the cows placed in ordinary circumstances on proper pasture.

As to the length of time that cows continue to give milk after going to the bull, M. Guenon's replies were, with a single exception, in conformity with the facts and his estimates of the butyraceous qualities of the milk were equally correct.

The results were altogether conclusive: they confirmed those already obtained in the presence of several agricultural societies, and particularly that were published after 248 trials, twenty months ago, by the Central Agricultural Society of the Lower Seine, whose president — M. Demoy — has a seat in this congress, and made one of your committee.

Several of your colleagues, and the reporter among them, has studied with more or less care the printed treatise, and acknowledged its general correctness; and one of them — M. Deffez (of Nerac) — who, under more favorable circumstances, and with the guidance of the author himself, had been enabled to study the theory practically, with stables and cattle fairs of the south, gave his estimate of the cows presented for trial, and these estimates, invariably in accordance with those of Mr. Guenon, proved the almost mathematical exactness of the principles upon which this singular and valuable system is based.

It is known that it is founded on the arrangement or disposition of the hair, in a space commencing at the upper extremity of the vulva, and descending to the roots of the teats, winding as it descends, covering the inner and hind parts of the thighs. It is from the arrangement of the hair in this space that the deductions are drawn as to the quantity, duration, and quality of the milk.

What are the mysterious relations existing between these external characters and the milk-producing organs? The author endeavors to explain, but his explanations only serve to justify the appeals that you have made on this body to the investigations of science.

The result would seem to be, from what precedes, that the application of Guenon's system can be made everywhere with the greatest facility, after reading his book; but it is due to truth to say that this is not the fact; that considerable difficulties are in the way of those who wish to turn it to account, and that some sagacity and perseverance are necessary to master it completely.

An honorable member who has your entire confidence, assures us that in his department where the system is generally applied, the number of bad milkers is diminishing in a striking manner, and that at the expense of surrounding departments, where their owners are compelled to seek less enlightened purchasers; and our president himself — the duke of Decazes — has stated that Guenon's method was being adopted with signal benefit in the southwest.

Admitted by our most learned veterinaries of the Royal College of Alfort and elsewhere, encouraged by the government, confirmed by a thousand proofs, and sanctioned by your approval, the discovery of Mr. Guenon may now be considered as having reached the dignity of a science. It applies alike to males and females — to calves and full-grown animals; and from this last fact we make this fruitful deduction: *Hereafter the farmer need rear none but such calves as will make good milkers, handing over to the butcher those that will not.*

Thus in a short time the daily production of milk in France may be increased by several millions of pints daily. Nor is this all. The abundance and quality of milk in the dams must contribute largely to the improvement of the progeny.

Mr. Guenon should receive a national remuneration, and be engaged to deliver lectures in the different Veterinary, Agricultural, and Normal schools of the kingdom, and in the presence of such societies as may call for him. These would be the speediest and best means of spreading the knowledge of this discovery, and it will no doubt be admitted that we can not be in too great haste to repair the time lost in ridicule, doubt, or indifference—the inevitable preface to all undertakings beneficial to humanity.

E. BARBIER,
Chairman of the Committee.

☞ This edition has also been improved by the addition of an interesting essay on *Spaying Milch Cows*, with the mode of operation.

PREFACE

BY THE AMERICAN EDITOR.

ALTHOUGH that portion of the matter, here offered to American farmers, which was translated for and originally published in the FARMERS' LIBRARY, might well be considered as worth the price of this volume, the Publishers have desired to render the work more acceptable and useful, by the addition of brief Introductory Sketches, descriptive of various Races of Cattle, as well as of Dairy Management, and of some of the Diseases to which *Cows and Calves* are particularly liable.

Most of these additions have been derived from CHAMBERS'S INFORMATION FOR THE PEOPLE; selected for the reason that, while they are deemed by the American Editor to be, generally, judicious and profound, the style is so plain and practical that "he who runs may read" and understand them. Remarks have been added by the Editor of the FARMERS' LIBRARY, where it was supposed they might be needed to adapt the work more perfectly to the use of American readers.

It has been truly observed that the most remarkable of all the changes and meliorations effected in cattle by the potent influence of domestication, the most marked improvement has been in the *capacity of the Cow for giving milk*. How much may not that capacity be enhanced now, by close attention to the milk-bearing signs or "escutcheons" so minutely described by M. GUENON?

By selecting for breeding stock, from generation to generation, such only as display these infallible indications, and condemning to the knife all that are devoid of them—supposing the system to be unerring as it has been pronounced by successive Committees appointed to investigate it—what is to prevent the establishment of a race as uniform and remarkable for excellence at the pail as the *Devon* Ox is for the yoke, or the courser of high-bred eastern extraction for the turf? and that, too, without recurrence to importation—seeing that, among our "country cows," individuals have been found equal, in yield of milk and butter, to any to be traced in the Herd-Book?—Instance the Cream-pot Breed, built up by Col. JACQUES, of Charlestown, Mass. whose calves are bespoken at $100; the celebrated middle-sized Oak's Cow, of Danvers, that gave, on evidence satisfactory to the Mass. Ag. Society, 484 pounds of butter from the 5th of April to the 25th of September, and, more recently, the wonderful Prize Cow, KAATSKILL, property of Mr. DONALSON, of Blithewood, New-York, which received the prize of the New-York State Agricultural Society, at Poughkeepsie, in 1844, on satisfactory evidence that she "yielded, when kept on grass only, 38¼ quarts of milk per day, and that, from the milk given by her in two days, 6¼ pounds of butter were made—being at the rate of 22¾ pounds per week."

When such cases turn up by chance, why, we repeat, may not a Breed of deep milkers be *established and relied upon* as confidently as it is known that "like produces like"? After all, now *that this discovery has been made*, and proclaimed, on the ground of repeated trials and testimony, to all appearance conclusive, what is there in the theory that lactiferous secretions should produce and show themselves in external marks and cutaneous exudations, any more wonderful or out of the way, than that other secretions and faculties are known to produce not only marked differences in *form* and *color*, but even perceptible, and, for the most part, offensive *effluvia?*

Observe the effect, in these respects, not only in the external differences of color and shape, which mark the different *sexes*, but the no less striking effects produced by early emasculation of the horse, the bull, the hog, and the goat! Hence, it is only "if I were *hungry*," says the Psalmist, "I will eat the flesh of *bulls*, and drink the blood of *goats*."

The famous Tuscany *Ox*, so celebrated for strength, activity, and endurance, and which Commodore JONES, in one of his letters addressed from the Mediterranean to Mr. SKINNER, says will travel 22 miles a day, with heavy loads of ship timber, is, all over, of uniform light grey color; but leave him unabridged of his full sexual proportions, and the effect is sure to be exhibited in the *black color and great enlargement of the neck, and curly forehead*. Is it, then, we repeat, extraordinary or incredible that the milky secretions of the Cow should produce, in the region where that process is carried on, and where her characteristic excellence lies, effects not more visible or striking than are produced on the *size, color and growth of the hair*, on the shoulders, neck and head of the bull? Are the external signs—the difference in the growth and curl of the hair, constituting the "escutcheons," and the scurf or dandruf thrown out on the skin, as described in this book—any more remarkable or strange in the one case than the other? But—"all things are strange"—*until they are found out!*

New-York, March, 1840.

REMARKS
AND
OBSERVATIONS ON THE COW
AND
THE DAIRY:
INTRODUCTORY TO GUENON'S TREATISE
ON MILCH COWS.

THE COW AND THE DAIRY.

Next to the horse, the COW is justly valued as the most useful animal which man has been able to domesticate and retain permanently in his service. The Ox tribe, of which it is the female, belongs to the order *Ruminantia*, in the class *Mammalia ;* these terms implying that the animals ruminate or chew their food a second time, and have mammæ or teats with which they suckle their young.— In the Ox tribe there are different genera and species, all more or less differing from each other.

The Wild Breed, from being untamable, can only be kept within walls or good fences; consequently, very few of them are now to be met with, except in the parks of some English gentlemen, who keep them for ornament and as a curiosity. Their color is invariably of a creamy white ; muzzle black ; the whole of the inside of the ear, and about one-third of the outside from the tip downward, red ; horn white, with black tips very fine, and bent upward ; some of the Bulls have a thin upright mane, about four or five inches long. The weight of the Oxen is from 450 to 550 lbs. and the Cows from 280 to 450 lbs. The beef is finely marbled and of excellent flavor.

Of the Domesticated Ox, the varieties from the effect of cultivation are now very numerous. The Ox, in one or other of its genera, and for the sake of its labor as a beast of draught, its flesh, or the milk of its female, has been domesticated and carefully reared from the earliest times—in some countries having been raised to the rank of a divinity, or, at least, held as an object of extreme veneration.

The domesticated species of Oxen is, in all its varieties, materially altered from its wild parentage. Influenced by climate, peculiar feeding, and training in a state of subjection, its bony structure is diminished in bulk and power, its ferocity tamed, and its tractability greatly improved. Our observations will refer chiefly to the Cow, on which very great changes have been effected by domestication : the most remarkable of these alterations has been in the *capacity for giving milk*. In a wild state, the udder is small, and shrinks into an insignificant compass when the duty of suckling is over ; but when domesticated for the sake of its milk, and that liquid is drawn copiously from it by artificial means, the lacteal or milk-secreting vessels enlarge, and the udder expands, so as to become a prominent feature in the animal. In this manner, by constant exercise, the economy of the cultivated species of Cows has been permanently altered, and rendered suitable to the demands which are constantly made on it. Yet it is important to remark that those milk-yielding powers are not equal in the different varieties or breeds of Cows. Some breeds, from the influence of circumstances, give a large quantity of milk, but of a thin or poor quality, while others yield less milk, but of a good or rich quality. Whether, then, the cow-keeper wish *quantity* or *quality*, is the question for him to solve in making a selection of stock. In general, near large towns, where the demand for milk is considerable, the object of dairymen is to keep Cows which will give a large quantity of milk, no matter of what sort. Private families in the country are usually more regardful of the quality of the article; they wish a little milk which is good, some fine cream, and perhaps, also, some sweet butter and cheese; and on that account are more careful in the choice of their Cows. For those who go for mere quantity, and yet have some honest scruples left about resorting to the *pump*, the old fashioned, large framed, big boned *Holderness* would do best; while for *cream* only, for family use, no breed can compare, in color and richness of milk, with the ewe-necked, deer-looking, ragged-boned *Alderney*. This breed may be seen at Roswell House, residence of Mr. Colt, Paterson, New-Jersey. The following is a list of breeds which may aid the selection of Cows in these different respects:

BREEDS OF CATTLE.

The breeds of cattle vary in different districts, from the small hardy varieties of the north Highlands, to the bulky and handsome breeds of the southern parts of England. It has been customary to classify the whole according to the comparative length of the horns—as the Long-Horned, Short-Horned, Middle-Horned, Crumpled-Horned, and Hornless or Polled breeds. Besides these, there are many intermixed breeds. The Middle-Horned Cows, which are found in the north of Devon, the east of Sussex, Herefordshire, and Gloucestershire, in England, are among the most valuable and beautiful varieties of the animal.

Whatever be the breed, there are certain conformations which are indispensable to the thriving, valuable Ox or Cow. If there is one part of the frame, the form of which, more than of any other, renders the animal valuable, it is the chest. There must be room enough for the heart to beat and the lungs to play, or sufficient blood for the purposes of nutriment and strength will not be circulated; nor will it thoroughly undergo that vital change which is essential to the proper discharge of every function. We look, therefore, first of all, to the wide and deep girth about the heart and lungs. We must have both: the proportion in which the one or the other may preponderate will depend on the service we require from the animal; we can excuse a slight degree of flatness of the sides, for he will be lighter in the forehand, and more active; but the grazier must have width as well as depth. And not only about the heart and lungs, but over the whole of the ribs, must we have both length and roundness; the *hooped* as well as the deep barrel is essential; there must be room for the capacious paunch—room for the materials from which the blood is to be provided. The beast should also be ribbed home; there should be little space between the ribs and the hips. This seems to be indispensable in the Ox, as it regards a good healthy constitution and a propensity to fatten; but a largeness and drooping of the belly, notwithstanding that the symmetry of the animal is not improved, are considered advantageous in the Cow, because room is thus left for the udder; and if these qualities are accompanied by swelling milk veins, her value in the dairy is generally increased. This roundness and depth of the barrel, however, are most advantageous in proportion as found behind the point of the elbow, more than between the shoulders and legs; or low down between the legs, rather than upward toward the withers; for the heaviness before, and the comparative bulk of the coarser parts of the animal, are thus diminished, which is always a very great consideration. The loins should be wide. Of this there can be no doubt, for they are the prime parts; they should seem to extend far along the back; and although the belly should not hang down, the flanks should be round and deep. Of the hips, it is superfluous to say that, without being ragged, they should be large; round rather than wide, and presenting, when handled, plenty of muscle and fat. The thighs should be full and long, close together when viewed from behind, and the farther down they continue close the better. The legs may occasionally vary in length according to the destination of the animal; but shortness is a good general rule, for there is an almost inseparable connection between length of leg and lightness of carcass, and shortness of leg and propensity to fatten. The bones of the legs (and they are taken as a sample of the bony structure of the frame generally) should be small, but not too small—small enough for the well-known accompaniment, a propensity to fatten—small enough to please the consumer; but not so small as to indicate delicacy of constitution and liability to disease. Lastly, the hide—the most important thing of all—should be thin, but not so thin as to indicate that the animal can endure no hardship; movable, mellow, but not too loose, and particularly well covered with fine and soft hair.

Of the various breeds and cross-breeds of Cows now in use, there are a few which enjoy the best reputation. We may name, for example, the *Old Yorkshire Stock*, a cross between the Teeswater and Holderness breed; the *Long-Horned* or *Lancashire breed*; the *Short-Horned* or *Dutch breed*; the *Middle-Horned breeds of Devonshire, Sussex*, and *Hereford*; the *Ayrshire breed*; the *Alderney breed*, &c. Some of these merit particular attention. We should first point to the

DEVONSHIRE Cow.—The Devonshire is a handsome breed of cattle, well set up on their legs, straight along the back, small muzzle, generally red in color, and, both as Oxen and Cows, they feed well at an early age. The Cow is much smaller than the Bull, but roomy for breeding, and is distinguished for her clear, round eye, and general loveliness and neatness of features. Fed on the fine pastures of North Devon, the Cow yields a rich quality of milk, and in reasonable

Devonshire Cow.

abundance. The North Devon breed prevails in some parts of Somersetshire, and has been introduced into other quarters of the country, but is not considered suitable in situations greatly differing from its native county as respects climate and herbage.

Incomparably the best herd of *Devons* in this, if not in any country, is the large one of GEORGE PATTERSON, Esq. near Sykesville, Md. Its excellence has been established and maintained by frequent importations of the best Bulls to be had in England, without limit as to cost, and by *invariably good keep:* The signs of genuineness and of excellence in the Devon are the absence, as near as possible, of *white* in any part, and a *yellow*, not *dark* skin showing itself around the eye and muzzle. The winner of successive prizes for best cheeses at the American Institute lately observed that he considered the Devon decidedly the best breed of cattle for the general purposes of New-England; while for his purpose exclusively, milk and cheese, he preferred a large infusion of Short-Horn blood.

HEREFORDSHIRE Cow.—The Hereford breed of cattle is larger than that of North Devon. It is broad across the hind quarters, narrow at the sirloin; neck and head well proportioned; horns of a medium size, turned up at the points; color deep red, but with face and some other parts generally white; and countenance cheerful and sagacious. This Cow is reckoned among the best in England as respects the production of milk, and, when too old for that purpose, it fattens to a greater weight than the North Devons. The *Herefords* have maintained a long and animated contest for superiority with the Short-Horns in England, and the Editor thinks (but mind, he can't be made to *enter into a contest* about it) it

INTRODUCTORY REMARKS:

Hereford Cow.

is rather gaining ground on its great rival. Has the latter any links yet to let out?

The GALLOWAY breed of cattle is well known for various valuable qualities, and easily distinguished by the want of horns. It is broad across the back, with a very slight curve between the head and quarters, broad at the loins, the whole body having a fine round appearance. The head is of a moderate size, with large rough ears, chest deep, legs short, and clean in the neck. The prevailing color is black, those of this color being thought the most hardy, although this varies. This breed is highly esteemed, as there is no other kind which arrives at maturity so soon, and their flesh is of the finest quality. The milk is very fine, but is not obtained in very large quantities. Great numbers of this breed are sent annually to Smithfield market; and it is remarkable that they are generally in as good condition after the journey as before. The Suffolk Dun, also a hornless breed, is supposed to be a variety of the Galloway, from their general resemblance.

The AYRSHIRE breed, which is considered the most valuable in Scotland, is of the small sized and middle horned race; its origin is unknown, as it has been long settled in the county from which it derives its name. In modern times, the

Ayrshire Bull.

breed has been improved by judicious selection, coupling, and general treatment. The common characteristics of this excellent variety of Cows are thus described by Mr. Aiton in his "Survey of Ayrshire:"—" Head small, rather long and narrow at the muzzle; eye small, smart, and lively; horns small, crooked, and set at considerable distances from each other; neck long, rather slender, tapering toward the head, with no loose skin below; shoulders thin; fore quarters light; hind quarters large; back straight, broad behind, the joints rather loose and open; carcass deep; legs small, short, with firm joints; udder capacious, stretching forward; the milk veins large and prominent; teats short, all pointing outward." The Ayrshire Cow is very docile, feeds well, is easily managed, and, as a dairy Cow, is equal to any other. It is inferior, however, for *feeding*, to the Devon, Sussex, and Hereford breeds. There have been several importations of Ayrshires —one some dozen years ago by A. J. DAVIE, of N. C. These we saw in Baltimore, as we have several other specimens there, and elsewhere. These were selected by Mr. D. in Scotland, and from their appearance, were, as we have thought, among the best specimens that have been brought to this country.— John Ridgely, Esq. of Hampton got this lot, and may, perhaps, have some of their descendants now. Dr. Hoffman more recently made an importation of choice individuals of this breed to Baltimore. Mr. Randall, of New-Bedford, Mass., has, perhaps, the largest herd of Ayrshires in this country. Several were imported into Massachusetts some years since, and our impression had been that they failed to establish themselves in the estimation of Yankee Farmers, yet the Massachusetts Agricultural Society lately invested a large portion of their funds in an importation of Ayrshires and North Devons, of which an account may be seen in the FARMERS' LIBRARY AND JOURNAL OF AGRICULTURE, November No. page 257 of the Journal. The specimens we have seen of Ayrshires appeared to be on the model, and with a good deal of the coat of the Short-Horn; the hair perhaps shorter, and in that, enabling them the better to bear *wet* weather. But they have the neat form of the Short-Horn only on a miniature scale when compared to them. Mr. STEVENSON, our late Minister to London, who passed all his leisure time among the noblemen and gentlemen Farmers in the best agricultural districts of England and Scotland, has some superior specimens of Ayrshires.

Ayrshire Cow.

Many of the Ayrshire Dairy Cows, when properly fed, will yield from six to eight gallons per day during a part of the summer. The quantity varies much during the year, from one and a half to six gallons or more; and the highest average of the milk yielded by this breed is one thousand gallons per annum. It is only some of the finest Cows that will yield such a quantity as this, and from five hundred to seven hundred and fifty gallons may be calculated as the most general yearly produce. Every two and one-third gallons of milk will afford one pound of butter, of sixteen ounces to the pound, or eight gallons will give three pounds. About twenty-six gallons of milk will give a stone of cheese, fourteen pounds to the stone, and a good milch Cow will thus yield thirty-six stones annually, which, at 10s. per stone, is £18 per annum for this article alone.

The SHORT-HORNED or Dutch breed is considered of great value, both for milking and feeding. There are many varieties of it, known by the names of the counties where they have been raised. The best of these varieties are large in the carcass, well proportioned, broad across the loins, chine full, legs short, head small but handsome, neck deep, but in keeping with the size of the body, color generally red and white mixed, or what is called flecked, hide thin. The flesh of this breed is thick, close-grained, retaining the juices well; and from this circumstance is in request for victualing ships going on long voyages.

Regarding the milking qualities of this breed, Mr. Dickson, an eminent cattle-dealer, who has had the most extensive experience throughout the whole country, says—"It has been frequently asserted that the Short-Horned Cows are bad milkers; indeed, that no sort of cattle are so deficient in milk. But this deficiency of milk does not proceed from the circumstance of the Cows being of the Short-Horned kind. Had the flesh been neglected as much as the milk by the eminent breeders, and the property of giving milk as much cherished as the development of flesh, the Short-Horned Cows would have been deep milkers. Indeed, it is not to be doubted that, where the general secreting powers of the animal system have been increased, the power of secreting milk will be increased with the power of secreting fat; all that seems requisite is to encourage the power of that secretion which is most wanted for the time. It would be to desire an impossibility to desire the full development of flesh, fat, and milk, at the same time; but there is no absurdity in desiring a large secretion of flesh and fat at one time, and a large secretion of milk at another, from the same Cow. Accordingly, this is the very character which has been acquired by Short-Horned Cows. They will yield from six to sixteen quarts a day throughout the season; and they are such constant milkers, that they seldom remain dry above six weeks or two months before the time of calving. I know a Scotch breeder who had a Short-Horned Cow which gave fifteen quarts a day during the flush of the grass in summer, and never went dry for two seasons. A cross between a Galloway Cow and a Short-Horned Bull in Berwickshire yielded twenty pints [twenty "*pints*" here probably mean *Scotch* pints, equal to English quarts] a day during the best of the season, and she had to be milked five times a day to keep her easy." We have thus considered it our duty to give the opinion of Mr. Dickson regarding the value of the Short-Horned breed of Cows as a dairy stock, seeing that the demand for Short-Horned Bulls has of late years been great in many of the counties of both England and Scotland. It seems, however, a well-confirmed opinion that the breed which of all others appears to be gaining ground, throughout the United Kingdom, for abundant produce on ordinary pasture, is the Ayrshire kyloe, which is described as without a parallel under a similar soil, climate, and relative circumstances, either for the dairy, or feeding for the shambles. But the ever variable circumstances in climate, soil, shelter, and the quality and quantity of the pasturage, as well as the winter feeding and general treatment, will always have an effect upon the stock.

Mr. GEORGE LAW, of Baltimore, has an imported Irish Short-Horn Cow, Sophy, sent to this country by Mr. MURDOCH, (now of N. C. near Asheville, a gentleman farmer of superior judgment and various intelligence,) which gave last summer, when well fed and in full milk, 38 quarts, or *one bushel of milk, a day*. Her "escutcheons" or signs correspond with those laid down in the work of M. GUENON, here in hand transferred from the FARMERS' LIBRARY.

In proof of our suggestion, that with the aid and close observance of the directions given in that work, a *milk*-race of the greatest excellence may be established on the basis of our country stock, we need only mention first the success of Col. JACQUES in the formation of his "*cream-pot*" breed. His calves of that blood are bespoken at $100—also the case of the Cow called "*the Oaks Cow*," which was of what is called the Country breed, and rather under size. It is not to be doubted, that if this great discovery in *kine-ology* had been made, she would have been found to display the "escutcheons," in full relief, and lastly to show, that for *milking* purposes, we need not go abroad, unless, as we go for foreign voters, for increase of numbers. We may refer to Mr. DONALDSON's famous Cow, *Kaatskill*, of which a fine portrait is given in the *Cultivator*, with the following account:—"'Kaatskill' received the first prize of the New-York State Agricultural Society as the best *Dairy* Cow exhibited at Poughkeepsie, in 1844. We are unable to refer to the original statement furnished the Society by Mr. DONALDSON in regard to the produce of this Cow, but can say that satisfactory evidence was given that she had yielded, when kept on grass only, thirty-eight and a half quarts of milk per day, and that from the milk given by her in two days, six and a half pounds of butter were made, being at the rate of twenty-two and three-fourths pounds per week. Her appearance fully corresponds with the account of her produce. It is proper to state, that while her milk was measured for the purpose of accurately ascertaining the quantity, she was milked four times every twenty-four hours." Kaatskill is represented as a "native," which we suppose means what is commonly called "country breed."

The IMPROVED KERRY is an Irish breed, of rather diminutive size, hardy, and which can subsist on scanty pasture. This renders them exceedingly well adapted for hilly pastures, and for cottagers who may not have the best food to offer their stock. Their milk and butter are rich in quality, and for their size they are good milkers. They are quiet enough when let alone; but, if the least irritated, no fence can contain them. The Irish Cows have improved very much of late years, in consequence of crossing; and they are now, in many respects, thought equal to the breeds of either England or Scotland.

The LONG-HORNED or Lancashire is distinguished by the length of its horns, the thickness of its hide, and the large size of its hoofs. It is far from being a handsome animal, nor is it held in very general estimation either for milking or feeding.

THE COW AND THE DAIRY.

HIGHLAND BREEDS.—The cattle of the Highlands of Scotland are of small bulk and very hardy. The most esteemed are those belonging to the Western Highlands and Isles, called the Argyleshire breed, and frequently *kyloes*. It is thought that this breed might be much improved by judicious crossing, as was seen in the case of the Ayrshire kyloe, formerly mentioned. This breed is rather handsome in appearance; the horns are long and upright, head large, neck short and deep, legs of a good length, and the beef is in general estimation. The cattle of the Highlands and Isles are bred on an extensive scale of farming for the purpose of sending to the southern markets. Small in size at first, they increase in bulk as they are transferred to a more genial climate and richer pasturage as they proceed southward, till, by annual stages, they reach the neighborhood of London, when they are large and heavy. The breeds may, therefore, be considered more an object of culture for the shambles than the dairy.

The ALDERNEY breed of cattle is awkwardly shaped, with short, bent horns, and light red, dun, or fawn-colored skins. The appetite of the Cow is voracious, and it yields little milk, but that is of an exceedingly rich quality, and the animal is on that account preferred by families who do not regard the expense of keep.

We once knew an honest dairy-woman maintain that the milk of *one Alderney* Cow would color the butter from the milk of seven common Cows, mixed with hers. The Alderney Bull is vicious and intractable, but nothing can equal the beautiful color and richness of the milk and cream from the Alderney Cow. Noblemen in England, some of them rich enough to give a guinea for a tea-spoonful of cream for their coffee, keep an Alderney in their magnificent parks, especially for the means of improving that delicious beverage—especially when made of *old Mocha*—such as was offered, and by her own fair hands administered to her friends by a lady of this City on New-Year's day, in lieu of hebetating *egg-nog*, and other inebriating liquors or liqueurs.

In adverting briefly to the properties of cattle, it will be advisable to describe the points by which they are characterized:

1. *The nose or muzzle.*—In the Devon, Hereford, and Sussex, the muzzle is preferred when of a clear golden color. When brown or dark, it is an indication that this breed has been crossed with some of the Welsh or other breeds.
2. *The forehead* should neither be narrow nor very broad—the eye prominent. The nostril between the eye and muzzle should be thin, which is particularly the case in the best breeds of the Devon cattle.
3. *The horns* should be thin, projecting horizontally from the head, and turning up at the tips, as in the breeds of the Devon, Sussex, and Hereford.
4. *The neck* should be neither long nor short, full at the sides and not too deep in the throat, coming out from the shoulders nearly level with the chine, with a thin dewlap.
5. *The top of the plate bones* should not be too wide, but rising upon a level with the chine, and well thrown back, so that there may be no hollowness behind; this point gives facility to the walk. From the point of the shoulder to the top of the plate bones should be rather full outside, to admit the ribs to bow.
6. *The shoulder point* should lay flat with the ribs without any projection. When the shoulder point projects outward, the beast seldom fattens well about the shoulder vein.
7. *The breast* should be wide and open, projecting forward.
8. *The chine* should lie straight, and well covered with flesh.

9. *The loin* should be flat and wide—the side lying parallel, and nearly as high as the chine—almost as wide at the fore as at the hinder part; being an indication of the ribs bowing out, which is desirable.
10. *The hip or huckle bones* should be wide apart, coming upon a level with the chine, to the first touch or setting on of the tail.
11. *The first touch or tip of the rump* should be tolerably wide, so that the tail drop in a level between the two points. The tail should come out broad, as an indication of a flat chine.
12. *The thigh* should not be too full outside nor behind, which is always an indication of bully flesh, but the inside or twist should be full.
13. *The hock or hough* should be flat and rather thin, not coarse and gummy, which indicates coarseness in the animal.
14. *The hind leg* should be flat and thin. The legs of a medium length, and the hock or hough rather turning out.
15. *The feet or claws* not too broad.
16. *The flank* should be full and heavy when the animal is fat, indicative of being fat inside.
17. *The belly* should not drop below the breast, but in a horizontal line with it.
18. *The brisket.*
19. *The shoulder* should be rather flat, not projecting.
20. *The foreleg* should be also flat and upright, but not fleshy.
21. *The round or pot-bone* should not project, but lie flat with the outside of the thigh.
22. *The under jaw.*—The jaws should be rather wide, particularly for beasts intended for working, as it affords them greater liberty to breathe.
23. *The chap* should be fine, indicating a disposition to feed.
24. *The ribs* should spring nearly horizontally from the chine, the sides round forming a circle; in which case the animal will never drop in the belly, and will lay its meat on the prime parts. The great objection to the Sussex breed of cattle is that they are too sharp in the chine, and the ribs too flat. When this is the case, the animal will always drop in the belly, and seldom lay its meat on the prime joints.

Remarks on Breeds.

We have thus briefly treated of some of the many breeds of cattle considered valuable as dairy stock in Britain; but we pretend not to give any decided opinion as to which is best. The merits of each kind have been vigorously contested by their respective advocates, and it would be extremely difficult to decide between them. Upon the form and qualifications of a perfect Cow, it ought to be observed, that whatever breed is selected, there is a wide difference between the form of one meant for fattening and that intended for the dairy. The first should resemble the Ox as nearly as possible; while the latter should be long and thin on the head, with a brisk, quiet eye, lank in the neck, narrow across the shoulders, but broad at the haunches; and there should be no tendency to become fat. The udder should be large and full looking, but not protruding too far behind; the teats all pointing out and downward, equal in size and rather long and tapering; all corresponding with the signs or escutcheons as given in this book. A Cow with a high back-bone, large head, small udder, and showing an inclination to become fat, will be found to be a bad milker. This description applies to all breeds; and of course the difference between a Cow for fattening and one for yielding milk will be comparative.

Mr. Aiton mentions the following as the most important qualities of the Dairy Cow:—" Tameness and docility of temper greatly enhance its value. One that is quiet and contented feeds at ease, does not break over fences, or hurt herself or other cattle, will always yield more milk than than those who are of a turbulent disposition. To render them docile, they ought to be gently treated, frequently handled when young, and never struck or frightened. Some degree of hardiness, however, a sound constitution, and a moderate degree of life and spirits, are qualities to be wished for in a milch Cow, and what those of Ayrshire generally possess. Some have thought that a Cow living on a small quantity of food was a valuable quality, but that will depend upon the quantity of milk given by the Cow that eats little compared with those that eat much. If the Cow that eats little gives as much milk as the one that eats more, it certainly is a valuable quality; but of this I entertain doubts, which forty years' experience and observation have served to confirm. Speculative writers affirm that some Cows will fatten as well, and yield as much milk, when fed on coarse as others will do on rich food. Cows that have been reared and fed on coarse pasture will yield some milk of a good quality, and from which the best butter may be extracted; while a Cow that has been reared and fed on much better pasture, would, if turned on that which is bad, give scarcely any milk. With persons living in towns and villages, and keeping but a single Cow, with opportunity of grazing on the commons, and depending mainly on them for food, a good rule is to get their Cow, not over the middle size; and from a poorer district of country. If she comes from rich, fertile pastures, she will fall off in her milk, below the quantity which he was assured she had been accustomed to give, and thus disappoint him. If from a poorer district, with the addition of the "slop" from the house and kitchen, and the *external signs here laid down*, she will be sure to improve. But if a Cow that has been accustomed to feed on bad pasture, be put on that which is better, she will greatly increase in milk, and fatten much faster. If two Cows of the same age and condition, and which have been reared and fed on food of equal quality, are put, the one on bad food, and the other on that which is good, the latter will yield four times the milk, and fatten four times faster than the former. A Cow need not always be fed on green clover, cabbages, and cauliflower; but she will neither fatten nor yield milk if she gets no better fare than rushes, bent, and sage grass."

A writer in the "Farmer's Magazine," a few years ago, presented the following doggrel lines, as combining what are popularly considered the good points of a Cow, such as is common among the Short-Horned breed of Yorkshire:—

> "She's long in her face, she's fine in her horn,
> She'll quickly get fat without cake or corn;
> She's clean in her jaws, and full in her chine,
> She's heavy in flank, and wide in her loin.
>
> She's broad in her ribs, and long in her rump,
> A straight and flat back, without e'er a hump;
> She's wide in her hips, and calm in her eyes,
> She's fine in her shoulders, and thin in her thighs.
>
> She's light in her neck, and small in her tail,
> She's wide in her breast, and good at the pail,
> She's fine in her bone, and silky of skin—
> She's a grazier's without, and a butcher's within."

To ensure the perpetuation of valuable qualities in Cows, it is necessary to breed from good Bulls of a similar variety to the Cows. The heifer or young Cow, if properly pastured, should begin to breed at two years, or not beyond two and a half years old. The Cow is at her prime at from four to six years, and declines into old age at ten or eleven years, when it is customary to fatten her for market. Dairymen, in selecting Cows, prefer those which have had their third or fourth calf when they have attained their fifth or sixth year. The Bull is in his prime at three years, and should not be used after eight or nine years old.

GENERAL MANAGEMENT OF COWS.

Calving.

The Cow goes with young nine calendar months, or 270 days but this length of time is liable to variation, from the effect of circumstances. A calf is most likely to survive and be healthy which has gone exactly the nine months. Cows come into season at different periods of the year, in which state they remain for a few days, after which the affection ceases, but it afterward returns in three or four weeks. The farmer watches these periods, and permits the company of the Bull at such a time as will produce the young at a time of the year when grass is plentiful for the nourishment of the mother. This should be an advanced period of Spring, for the Cow will require nourishing diet some time before she drops her calf as well as afterward.

A Cow may be kept in milk up to the time of her calving, by daily taking a quantity from her; but this is most injurious to the fœtus, [that depends on the external signs—see the *Cow Book!*] and the excitement of the new upon the old milk is apt to produce local inflammation. In towns, where dairymen care nothing for the calf, and must have milk at all risks, Cows are often maltreated by being milked to the last; but no one who conducts a dairy on proper principles will be guilty of this inhumanity. The best plan is to allow the Cow to go gradually dry, and not milk her at all for six or eight weeks before calving. This will keep her in a reasonably good condition, and save extra food, which it is not advantageous to give on a luxuriant scale, because high feeding at this period may induce inflammation and fever at calving.

No animal is so liable to abortion as the Cow; it takes place at uncertain periods during the pregnancy; sometimes it occurs from fright, teazing by other cattle in the field, or over-high condition; but also not unfrequently from some bad habit acquired by the animal. It has been found that the habit is infectious; and when once it has got among a parcel of Cows, it can be banished only with the greatest difficulty. In all cases the aborted fœtus should be buried deep and far from the Cow pasture; the Cow physiced, and its parts washed with chloride of lime; the Cow-house thoroughly lime-washed and otherwise purified; and lastly, the Cow fattened and sent to market.

If in a state of health, no difficulty will occur at the parturition; but should the case be otherwise, we prefer leaving the Cow-keeper to ask assistance from a person of practical skill, or veterinary surgeon, than to offer any speculative advices on the subject. With respect to the treatment after calving, we beg to quote the following directions from the volume on Cattle, " Library of Useful Knowledge:"—" Parturition having been accomplished, the Cow should be left quietly with the calf; the licking and cleaning of which, and the eating of the placenta, if it is soon discharged, will employ and amuse her. It is a cruel thing to separate the mother from the young so soon; the Cow will pine, and will be deprived of that medicine which Nature designed for her in the moisture which hangs about the calf, and even in the placenta itself; and the calf will lose that gentle friction and motion which help to give it the immediate use of all its limbs, and which, in the language of Mr. Berry, 'increases the languid circulation of the blood, and produces a genial warmth in the half-exhausted and chilled little animal.' A warm mash should be put before her, and warm gruel, or water from which some of the coldness has been taken off. Two or three hours afterward, it will be prudent to give an aperient drink, consisting of a pound of Epsom salts and two drachms of ginger. This may tend to prevent milk fever and garget in the udder. Attention should likewise be paid to the state of the udder. If the teats are sore, and the bag generally hard and tender, she should be gently but carefully milked three or four times every day. The natural and the effectual preventive of this, however, is to let the calf suck her at least three times in the day, if it is tied up in the Cow-house, or to run with her in the pasture, and take the teat when it pleases. The tendency to inflammation of the udder is much diminished by the calf frequently sucking; or should the Cow be feverish, nothing soothes or quiets her so much as the presence of the little one."

The Calf.

The Calf, when first dropped, is generally cleansed by the tongue of its dam from the slimy matter which always adheres to the skin of the animal. Sometimes it happens that the Cow will not at first recognize her offspring; but upon a small quantity of salt being strown over it, to which all neat cattle are particularly partial, she commences the motherly duties by licking the skin. The first milk appears to be calculated to nourish the Calf, which it should be allowed to suck plentifully before the Cow is milked. It is the practice with some, as soon as the Calf has sucked as much as it pleases, to milk the remainder so as to cleanly drain the udder, and give it to the Cow as nourishment.

The treatment of Calves in rearing varies materially in different counties, and even in districts. In Sussex, England, the Calf is by many not allowed to take all the milk of the Cow, but is shut up from her in the morning and evening, and a small quantity of bran or ground oats given in a trough, and not suffered to suck till the maid comes to milking, when she milks two speens, while the Calf sucks the other two; after which, when the girl has got all the milk she can, the Calf is left with the Cow a short time, to draw the udder as clean as possible; and if there be any lumps occasioned by the pores being stopped, through which the milk flows to the speens, the Calf, by sucking, will disperse them better than by any other means. Cows are frequently injured in their milk by not having their udders thoroughly cleansed for the first fortnight or three weeks after calving.— When the Calf is about a month old, it is suffered to run with the Cow in the day, and kept from her in the night. A portion of the milk is taken from the Cow, and the remainder is left for the Calf, which is again permitted to remain with her during the day: this practice is followed by some till the Calf is weaned. Some let the Calves go with the Cows when three or four weeks old, at which time the Cow has not a greater supply than sufficient for the Calf alone; after which it is allowed to run with the Cow till about twelve weeks, when it is weaned, and put in a confined place out of sight and hearing, to prevent the Cow being made uneasy from hearing her Calf. The Calf is then fed on cut grass, clover, or other green food, with hay and bran, till such time as it forgets its dam. It should then be turned out upon good pasture; for, unless the Calf be well fed at an early age, it will become stinted in its growth, and, when arrived at maturity, will not fatten so readily as if proper attention had been paid to it while young.

In many dairy districts, it has been found desirable to deprive the Calf of the greater portion of milk; which has been accomplished by its being taught to drink skimmed milk in a lukewarm state, by the following means:—When the animal has fasted two or three hours, the first and second fingers of the right hand are presented to its mouth; of these it readily takes hold, sucking very eagerly; in the mean time, a vessel of lukewarm milk is placed and supported by the left hand under the Calf's mouth; and, while it is sucking, the right hand is gradually sunk a little way into the milk, so that it may draw in a sufficient quantity without stopping the nostrils. Should, however, either from accident or from too sudden precipitation of the hand into the milk, the Calf let go its hold, the attempt must be repeatedly renewed till crowned with success. For the space of three or four weeks, they are usually fed with lukewarm milk and water. A small quantity of hay, ground oats or bran, and sometimes oil-cake, is then placed within their reach, which induces them to eat. Toward the end of May they are turned out to grass, being taken in for a few nights, when they have tepid milk and water given them; which is usually continued, though gradually, in smaller proportions during the last month, till they are able to feed themselves, when they totally disregard it. It is then advisable to turn them into pastures where the grass is short and sweet.

Many attempts have been made to rear Calves by artificial means, which by some is said to have answered very well, where the animal has been confined and shut up in the dark; this practice has been proved to be injurious, and especially if the Calves are intended for stock. We certainly have no practice which can answer so well as that where the laws of Nature are strictly attended to, and the Calf is supplied with nourishment such as Nature dictates.

The greatest attention in fattening Calves should be paid to cleanliness, without which neither will the Calf fatten quickly, nor when fat be of good color; much risk will also follow in losing the Calf from fever, or from scouring. Chalk should be always before them to lick, to counteract the acidity always found in great abundance in the stomach of the Calf when feeding on milk.

It is advisable in fattening Calves to keep them quiet, and to allow them to suck the Cow night and morning, taking the last of the milk, which is considered to be the most rich and nourishing. By this treatment the Calf will gradually become sufficiently fat in seven or eight weeks; and, when so, it is no advantage to keep it a day longer—as small veal, if fat, is preferable to large.

It is by some a practice to bleed Calves weekly, after they are four or five weeks old, and always a short time before they are killed—by which course the veal is rendered whiter.

As castrating Calves is an operation which ought not to be performed but by skillful practitioners, we shall refrain from giving any directions—recommending the operation to be performed at the age of eight or ten weeks, as at that age the danger is considerably lessened. The animals should be kept quiet and warm after the operation; and if, on the following day, the scrotum should be much swollen and inflamed, the wound may be opened, and the coagulated blood removed.

Whether calves are kept for veal or for stock, they are begun to be fed in the same manner, by sucking milk from a dish. As they naturally seek for the teat when their nose is put to the dish, the fingers of the attendant may be put into their mouth when in the milk, and this will set them going in the art of artificial sucking. "The milk" (says the author of "Clerical Economics,") "should be given to them sparingly at first, to render their appetite more keen, and prevent them from loathing at their food. For the first two weeks they should be fed on the milk first drawn from the Cow, locally termed the *forebroads*, which abounds with serum; and as they grow up, the quantity of milk is gradually increased to as much as the calves can be made to drink. After the first two or three weeks, by all means give them plenty of milk, warm from their mother; and let it be that which is last drawn from the Cow, locally termed *afterings*, which are much richer. Keep abundance of dry litter under them. Have them in a place that is well aired, and of a uniform temperature, neither too hot nor too cold; let the apartment be quite dark, excepting when the door is opened to give them food. If they enjoy the light, they become too sportive, and will not fatten. Take care that they are fastened to the wall, in such a way, by "swivels," that they cannot hang themselves. Never let them make their escape at the door, or, by their running and jumping, they will do more injury to themselves in three minutes than a week's feeding will make up. Don't keep them till they become too old, because, when they begin to grow to the bone, they require more milk than the manse can generally produce; and whenever they cease to advance in the fattening process, they begin to recede, and the milk for a week or two is lost. They should be kept from four to seven weeks, according as milk may be abundant and rich. If a calf be kept long, during the last two or three weeks, it will require the richest part of the milk of at least two or three Cows to bring it to the highest pitch of fatness. When the milk begins to fall short of the calf's appetite, some mix eggs and others peas-meal into their food; others try infusions of hay, oil-cake, and linseed; but none of these additions are approved of by those who feed calves to the greatest perfection. Meal is understood to darken the flesh, web, and lights of the animal; but sago has of late years been almost, from the first two or three weeks, boiled and mixed in its liquid state with the milk, and to great advantage. Begin with a saucerful of it or so, and gradually increase the quantity. Calves are very fond of chalk, and they also feel the want of salt.

Cow-House—Cleaning.

The Cow-house should be airy, and well ventilated; of moderate temperature, and kept very clean. The stalls for the Cows should be paved with smooth stones, slope gently toward the foot, where there should be a clear run of a gutter to carry off the urine to a pit outside. The stalls must be daily scraped and swept, and all refuse carried out to the dung-heap. In general, far too little litter is allowed. The Cow should have plenty of straw bedding, kept in a cleanly condition; and this, when soiled, is to be mixed with the dung for manure. The only fastening for the Cow should be a chain to go round the neck, with the other end round an upright post, but easily movable up and down, and allowing room for the animal shifting its position. The feeding manger or stone trough is on the ground, and ought to be kept free of all impurities; for though the Cow is not so nice as the horse, it has a disinclination for food not fresh and cleanly.

Except in dairies of a high order, it is customary to keep Cows in a shamefully unclean condition. The floor of their habitation is filthy, the walls ragged and full of vermin, and the hides of the animals dusty or barkened with dirt. Persons who keep Cows are not aware of the loss they incur from allowing them to live in this uncleanly state. Some people seem to think that they do quite enough for their Cows if they give them food and shelter; but besides this, they require to be kept very cleanly, though seldom indulged in that luxury. The Cow should be curried daily like the Horse; its hide should be freed from all impurities, and relieved from every thing that causes uneasiness. When you see a Cow rubbing itself against a post, you may depend on it that the animal is ill kept, and requires a good scrubbing. Irritation of the skin from impurities also causes them to lick themselves, a habit which is injurious, for the hairs taken into the stomach form a compact round mass, which may destroy the animal. If well curried, any danger from this catastrophe is avoided, the health is generally improved, and this improves the quality of the milk, besides increasing the quantity. A cottager might easily make two or three shillings more of his Cow weekly by attention to this point; and if he at the same time took pains to preserve all the liquid refuse of the cow-house, he might double that amount. How strange to reflect that many decent and well-meaning, but ignorant and rather lazily-disposed people, are suffering a loss of four or five shillings weekly from no other cause than this! It is long, however, before old habits are eradicated, and new and better ones introduced.

Feeding.

The Cow requires to be supplied with an abundance of food, not to make her fat, which is not desirable, but to keep up a regular secretion of milk in the system. The feeding must be regular, from early morning to night, and pure water must also be offered at proper intervals, if the Cow has not the liberty of going to the water herself.

Regarding the nature of the food of Cows, although soiling, or artificial feeding in the house, is at all times economical, there can be no doubt that the best milk and butter are produced by Cows fed on natural pasture; and, although the quantity of milk is not so great, yet the butter has a sweet taste, never to be discovered in the produce of soiled Cows. It was formerly the case in Scotland, and the practice is still continued in some parts, to put the Cows out to grass in spring in such an emaciated state that a considerable part of the best season was gone before they yielded the quantity of milk they would otherwise have done. On well-enclosed farms, it is the custom of many to keep their Cows out both night and day, from May till the end of October, so long as a full bite can be obtained; and some bring them into the house twice a day to be milked. Soiling, or feeding entirely in the house or court-yard, is but seldom practiced, except by some farmers in arable districts. Although complete soiling is only occasionally resorted to, yet a considerable quantity of rich green food is served out to the dairy stock in their stalls at night, and in the heat of the day, by such farmers as bring their Cows into the house at these times. This mode of feeding is more especially followed when the pasture begins to fail; the second crops of clover and tares, cabbages, coleworts, and other garden produce, are all given to the Cows in the house at this period. It is upon this system that the whole perfection of the Flemish husbandry is founded; and it could be put in practice, with the most beneficial results, in many other countries. In Holland, the Cows, when fed in the house, have their drink of water invariably mixed with oil-cake, rye, or oat-meal. Dairy Cows are allowed to be much injured by being denied a due supply of salt, which is said to improve the quality and increase the quantity of the milk. In the best managed dairies in Scotland, when the Cows are taken in for the winter, they are never put out to the fields until spring, when the grass has risen so much as to afford a full bite. In the moorish districts, however, they are put out to the fields for some hours every day when the weather will permit. In these districts, the winter food is turnips with marsh meadow hay—occasionally straw and boiled chaff.

In the richer districts, turnips and straw are given, and occasionally some clover hay in spring, or when the Cows have calved. Upon this subject nothing need be added, but that the quantity and quality of the milk will be in proportion to the nourishment in the food. White turnips afford a good quantity of milk, but they impart a very disagreeable taste, which may be removed, however, by steaming or boiling the turnips, or by putting a small quantity of dissolved saltpetre into the milk when new drawn. The quality of the milk depends a great deal on the Cow; influenced, however, by the food she eats. Linseed, peas and oat-meal produce rich milk; and a mixture of bran and grains has been recommended as food in winter. Brewers' grains are said to produce a large quantity of milk, but very thin—the quality being somewhat similar to that sold in large towns, yielding neither good cream nor butter. It has been found of some importance to feed Cows frequently—three or four times a day in summer, and five or six in winter—and to give them no more at a time than they can eat cleanly.

What has been stated regarding the feeding of Cows applies principally to those kept on dairy farms. In establishments for the supplying of large towns with milk, the method of feeding is somewhat different; there the practice is to feed them chiefly on distillers' wash, brewers' grains, and every sort of liquid stuff that will produce a large quantity of milk, without reference to its quality. The Edinburgh cow-keepers begin to feed with grain, dreg, and bran, mixed together, at five o'clock in the morning; feed again at one o'clock in the afternoon, and a third time at seven or eight o'clock in the evening; grass in summer, and turnips and potatoes in winter, being given in the two intervals. The grass is laid upon the straw, in order to impart to it a certain flavor, and make it palatable: it is eaten after the grass; and, in winter, straw or hay is given after the turnips. Part of the turnips and potatoes are boiled, particularly when there is a scarcity of grains.

The following is mentioned in the "Farmer's Magazine," as an improved mode of feeding milch Cows, near Farnham, in Surrey:—" Go to the cow-stall at six o'clock in the morning, winter and summer; give each Cow half a bushel of the mangel-wurzel, carrots, turnips, or potatoes, cut; at seven o'clock, the hour the dairy-maid comes to milk them, give each some hay, and let them feed till they are *all* milked. If any Cow refuses hay, give her something she will eat—such as grains, carrots, &c.—during the time she is milking, as it is *absolutely necessary* the Cow should feed while milking. As soon as the woman has finished milking in the morning, turn the Cows into the airing ground, and let there be plenty of *fresh water* in the troughs; at nine o'clock, give each Cow three gallons of the mixture (as under—to eight gallons of grains, add four gallons of bran or pollard); when they have eaten that, put some hay into the cribs; at twelve o'clock, give each three gallons of the mixture as before. If any Cow looks for more, give her another gallon. On the contrary, if she will not eat what you give her, take it out of the manger; for never at one time let a Cow have more than she will eat up *clean*. Mind and keep your mangers clean, that they do not get sour. At two o'clock, give each Cow half a bushel of carrots, mangel-wurzel, or turnips; look the turnips, &c. over well, before you give them to the Cows—as one rotten turnip, &c. will give a bad taste to the milk, and most likely spoil a whole dairy of butter. At four o'clock, put the Cows into the stall to be milked; feed them on hay as you did at milking-time in the morning, keeping in mind that the Cow, while milking, must feed on something. At six o'clock, give each Cow three gallons of the mixture as before. Rack them up at eight o'clock. Twice in a week, put into each Cow's feed at noon a quart of malt-dust."

Milking.

"Cows are milked twice or thrice a day, according to circumstances. If twice, morning and night; if thrice, morning, noon, and night. They should not go too long unmilked, for, independently of the uneasiness to the poor animal, it is severely injurious.

The act of milking is one which requires great caution; for, if not carefully and properly done, the quantity of the milk will be diminished, and the quality inferior, the milk which comes last out of the udder being always the richest.— It should, therefore, be thoroughly drawn from the Cows until not a drop more can be obtained, both to ensure a continuance of the usual supply of milk, and also to get the richest which the Cows afford. Cows should be soothed by mild usage, especially when young; for to a person whom they dislike, they never give their milk freely. The teats should always be clean washed before milking, and when tender, they ought to be fomented with warm water. The milking and management of the Cow should, in these circumstances, be only entrusted to servants of character, on whom the utmost reliance can be placed. In some places, it is a common practice to employ men to milk the Cows, an operation which seems better fitted for females, who are likely to do the work in a more gentle and cleanly manner, which is of essential importance.

The writer in the "Farmer's Magazine," above quoted, gives the following explicit directions to the dairy-maid in regard to milking:—" Go to the Cow-stall at seven o'clock; take with you *cold water* and a sponge, and wash each Cow's udder clean before milking; dowse the udder well with *cold* water, winter and summer, as it braces and repels heats. Keep your hands and arms clean. Milk each Cow as dry as you can, morning and evening, and when you have milked each Cow as you *suppose* dry, begin again with the Cow you first milked, and drip them each; for the principal reason of Cows failing in their milk is, from negligence in not milking the Cow dry, *particularly* at the time the calf is taken from the Cow. Suffer no one to milk a Cow but yourself, and have no gossiping in the stall. Every Saturday night give in an exact account of the quantity of milk each Cow has given in the week."

THE DAIRY.

The dairy should be cool, airy, dry, and free from vermin of all kinds. To prevent the intrusion of flies, the windows or ventilators ought to be covered with a fine wire gauze. The floor should be laid with smooth glazed tiles, and also the lower part of the walls; the benches on which the milk pans are to be placed are best when made of stone or slate, and about thirty inches broad. The ceiling should be at least eight feet from the floor, and finished in every respect like that of an ordinary dwelling-house. A slate roof is preferable to one of tile, as it tends to keep the temperature more equable. Cleanliness is of the most essential consequence in dairy management, and, if not strictly looked after, may cause considerable loss. It is this which has raised the produce of the dairies of Holland so much in public estimation. Every article in which milk is placed, more especially when made of wood, ought to be washed in boiling water, with a little soda or lime dissolved in it. If milk should happen to sour in any dish, the acid thus generated will injure any which may be afterward put into it; but if washed in water in which an alkali has been dissolved, the acid will be destroyed.

The utensils of a dairy are very numerous. The principal are milk-pails, shallow coolers for holding the milk, sieves for straining it through after it is taken from the Cow, dishes for skimming the cream, churns for making the butter, scales, weights, &c. For making cheese, there are likewise ladders, vats, tubs, curd-breakers, and presses; and various other articles will be required, which it is almost impossible to enumerate. The majority of them are made of wood; but in some of the best dairies in England and Scotland, it is now the practice to have the coolers made of cast-iron, wood lined with tin in the inside, or glazed earthenware. Maple is the wood generally used in England for the manufacture of these dishes; both from its lightness, and being easily cut, it can be finished in a neater style. In Holland, the milk-dishes are very commonly made of brass; and certainly brass or iron is to be preferred to wood, because the dishes made from either of these materials are more durable, and can be easier cleaned. It has been objected to earthenware vessels, that, being glazed with lead, the acid of the milk acting upon the glaze forms a very noxious poison. This, however, is scarcely correct; it would require a much stronger acid than that of milk to decompose the glaze. Zinc pans are now coming into use, and they can be safely recommended for their cool and cleanly qualities, besides being economical. We have seen it stated that cream rises best in zinc pans.

Churning is now, in all large dairy establishments, performed by machinery, worked either by horse or water power. Churns vary in size from ten to fifty, and even one hundred gallons, according to the size of the establishment. Great care should be taken to wash churns thoroughly with boiling water both immediately after they have been used, and before they are again to be put in operation; and those churns which admit of being easily cleaned are always to be recommended, even although they should not be so elegant in construction.

DAIRY PRODUCE.

Milk.

Milk consists of three materials blended together—called, in Science, the butteraceous, lactic, and serous kinds of matter—which can be separated by artificial means, so as to form *butter*, the milk called *buttermilk*, and *serum* or *whey*.—The whey is little else than water, slightly saline, and is generally the chief ingredient in the milk. When taken from the Cow, milk should be removed to the dairy or milk-house, and, after being sieved, placed in shallow pans, to throw up the butteraceous matter termed cream, which, being lightest, floats on the top.

The following observations on milk and its management, made by Dr. Anderson, are worthy of the consideration of cow-keepers:

"Of the milk drawn from any Cow at one time, that part which comes off at the first is always thinner, and of a much worse quality for making butter, than that afterward obtained; and this richness continues to increase progressively to the very last drop that can be obtained from the udder.

"If milk be put into a dish, and allowed to stand till it throws up cream, the portion of cream rising first to the surface is richer in quality and greater in quantity than that which rises in a second equal space of time; and the cream which rises in the second interval of time is greater in quantity and richer in quality than that which rises in a third equal space of time; that of the third is greater than that of the fourth, and so of the rest; the cream that rises continuing progressively to decrease in quantity, and to decline in quality, so long as any rises to the surface.

"Thick milk always throws up a much smaller proportion of the cream which it actually contains than milk that is thinner; but the cream is of a richer quality; and, if water be added to that thick milk, it will afford a considerably greater quantity of cream, and consequently more butter, than it would have done if allowed to remain pure; but its quality is, at the same time, greatly debased.

"Milk which is put into a bucket or other proper vessel, and carried in it to a considerable distance, so as to be much agitated, and in part cooled, before it be put into the milk-pans to settle for cream, never throws up so much or so rich cream as if the same milk had been put into the milk-pans directly after it was milked.

"From these fundamental facts, the reflecting dairyist will derive many important practical rules. Some of these we shall enumerate, and leave the rest to be discovered. Cows should be milked as near the dairy as possible, in order to prevent the necessity of carrying and cooling the milk before it is put into the creaming dishes. Every Cow's milk should be kept separate till the peculiar properties of each are so well known as to admit of their being classed, when those that are most nearly allied may be mixed together. When it is intended to make butter of a very fine quality, reject entirely the milk of all those Cows which yield cream of a bad quality, and also keep the milk that is first drawn from the Cow at each milking entirely separate from that which is last obtained, as the quality of the butter must otherwise be greatly debased, without materially augmenting its quantity. For the same purpose, take only the cream that is first separated from the first drawn milk. Butter of the very best quality can only be economically made in those dairies where cheese is also made; because in them the best part of each Cow's milk can be set apart for throwing up cream —the best part of this cream can be taken in order to be made into butter—and the remainder or all the rest of the milk and cream of the dairy can be turned into cheese. The spontaneous separation of cream, and the production of butter, are never effected but in consequence of the production of acid in the milk.— Hence it is that, where the whole milk is set apart for the separation of cream, and the whole of the cream is separated, the milk must necessarily have turned sour before it is made into cheese; and no very excellent cheese can be made from milk which has once attained that state."

We now pass on to a consideration of the most valuable ingredient in the dairy produce—

Butter.

Butter is made of cream, freed from its milky and serous properties. This is effected by churning. Some imagine that no butter can be good except such as is made from fresh cream; but this is a mistake, as cream requires to have a little acidity before the butter will form. The length of time which the cream should stand before churning has never been clearly ascertained; from three to seven days, however, may be considered as the proper period. A more important matter than the length of time which cream requires to stand, is the degree of temperature at which the cream will turn into butter. This has been ascertained from experiment to be from 45 to 75° of Fahrenheit. In Holland, when the cream is too cold, hot water is put into the churn to raise the temperature to 70 or 75°. The best quality of butter is obtained at a temperature of 51° according to experiments performed by Mr. Pooler; and the greatest quantity at a temperature of 56°. During the process of churning, the agitation will increase the heat to about five degrees more than it was when the cream was put into the churn. Mr. Pooler is of opinion, that the greater quantity of butter is obtained by the increased heat causing more milk to remain among the butter; and this, of course, must decrease its quality.

In some of the dairies in the neighborhood of Edinburgh, and in all those near Glasgow, the butter is made by churning the cream and the milk together. This is done in order to obtain the buttermilk, the demand for which is always great in large cities. When the milk and cream are to be churned together, the milk is kept in the coolers for from twelve to twenty-four hours, and then poured into a milk-tub. It remains here until required for churning; and will, during this time, have coagulated. If a certain quantity of milk is put into the milk-tub, and has coagulated before any more has creamed, the coagulated milk must in no way be disturbed, or, if the two quantities are mixed together, too much fermentation may be the consequence. The milk is not churned till it has become acid; and when once coagulation has taken place, it should be churned as early as convenient. If the milk has not fermented before churning, the buttermilk will keep for a much longer time, will have an agreeable taste, and will bear to be mixed with a little water. When the milk has fermented before being churned, the buttermilk will never be so good, nor will it keep for such a length of time as the former.

The operation of churning, whether it be of cream alone, or cream and milk, is performed in the same manner. The milk requires more time than cream to complete the process, from two to three hours being considered necessary, while cream alone may be effectually churned in an hour and a half. It is necessary that the operation should be slow in warm weather; for if done too hastily, the butter will be soft and white. If the cream is at too high a temperature, the churn should be cooled with cold spring water, to reduce it to the proper degree of heat. In winter, again, the operation of churning should be done as quickly as possible, the action being regular; and the churn should be warmed, to raise the temperature of the milk or cream. The air which is generated in the churn should be allowed to escape, or it will impede the process by the froth which it creates.

After the churning is performed, the butter should be washed in cold spring water, with a little salt in it, two or three times, to extract all the milk which may be lodging about the mass. It is said by some that the butter retains its sweetness much longer when no water is used; and others affirm that the washing improves the flavor. The extraction of the milk from butter will reduce its weight; but it appears from the experiments of Mr. Pooler upon the temperature of the cream, that the less milk which is in the butter its quality is proportionably improved. Kneading and beating the butter too much render it tough and gluey. After the milk has been carefully extracted, if the butter is to be salted, it should be mixed with the finest salt, in the proportion of ten ounces to fourteen pounds, more or less, according to the time the butter is to be preserved. The butter and salt should be well mixed together with the hand; and in Ireland it is customary to add a little saltpetre. A compound of one part of sugar, one part nitre and two parts of the best Spanish salt, finely powdered together, has been highly recommended for preserving butter. It is used in the proportion of one ounce to the pound; and it is said to give a flavor to the butter which no other kind ever acquires.

For making butter casks or kegs the wood of trees containing no acid is recommended. When wood contains acid it acts powerfully upon the salt in the butter, converting it into brine. Any wood will answer if boiled for a few hours, for by this process the pyrolignous acid will be entirely taken out.

In salting, the butter should never be put into the firkins in layers; but the surface should be left every day rough and broken, so as to unite better with that of the succeeding churning. The quality may likewise be better preserved by covering it over with a clean linen cloth dipped in pickle, and placing it in a cool situation.

Buttermilk.

This is the liquid which remains in the churn after removing the butter. If skimmed milk has been employed for churning, the buttermilk is thin, poor, and easily sours; but if from the churning of the entire milk, the buttermilk is more thick and rich, and is considered by many a delicious beverage. Good buttermilk is at all events exceedingly wholesome and nutritious. In Ireland it is largely used at meals with potatoes; in Scotland it is more frequently employed as a relish with oat-meal porridge; and for this purpose large quantities are brought to Edinburgh, Glasgow and other towns, from the adjoining rural districts. In

England, the buttermilk of farmers is usually employed in feeding pigs. In New-York it is always found for sale at the markets at from two to three cents per quart.

Devonshire Clouted Cream.

This is a preparation of the rich milk of Devonshire, and may be said to be a kind of half-formed butter, such is the solidness of its consistency. In Vancouver's "Survey of Devonshire," the following is described as the mode of preparing this delicious article:—" The milk is put into tin or earthen pans, holding about ten or twelve quarts each. The evening's meal is placed the following morning, and the morning's milk is placed in the afternoon, upon a broad iron plate heated by a small furnace, or otherwise over stoves, where exposed to a gentle fire, they remain until after the whole body of cream is supposed to have formed upon the surface; which being gently removed by the edge of a spoon or ladle, small air-bubbles will begin to rise, that denote the approach of a boiling heat, when the pans must be removed from off the heated plate or stoves. The cream remains upon the milk in this state until quite cold, when it may be removed into a churn, or, as is more frequently the case, into an open vessel, and then moved by the hand with a stick about a foot long, at the end of which is fixed a sort of peel from four to six inches in diameter, and with which about twelve pounds of butter may be separated from the buttermilk at a time—the butter in both cases being found to separate much more freely, and sooner to coagulate into a mass, than in the ordinary way, when churned from raw cream that may have been several days in gathering; and at the same time will answer a more valuable purpose in preserving, which should be first salted in the usual way, then placed in convenient-sized egg-shaped earthen crocks, and always kept covered with a pickle, made strong enough to float and buoy up about half out of the brine a new-laid egg. This cream, before churning, is the celebrated clouted cream of Devon."

Cheese.

Cheese may be made from cream alone, or from the whole milk; the object in either case being in the first place to separate the serum from the other materials. This is effected by curding the cream or milk, by the infusion of an acid, the refuse being tho serum or whey, which is of scarcely any value. [For a very valuable Treatise on the best mode of manufacturing Cheese, see FARMERS' LIBRARY AND MONTHLY JOURNAL OF AGRICULTURE, Vol. 1. pp. 137—150.]

LONDON DAIRY MANAGEMENT.

The quantity of fresh milk annually consumed in the British metropolis was lately calculated to be 39,420,000 quarts, costing £985,500, and being the produce of 12,000 Cows, kept principally in large dairy establishments in all parts of the environs. The milk is generally of the best kind when drawn from the animals; but, between the dairy and the consumer, it passes through several hands, each of whom takes a profit upon it, and increases the quantity of salable liquid by large infusions of water, chalk, &c. In the condition it usually reaches the public, it is shamefully adulterated. The charge of deteriorating the quality of the article is seldom made upon the cow-keepers, whose establishments are, for the most part, models of good management. As it may be interesting to our readers to have some account of these large dairies, we present the following particulars:

The two largest dairy establishments are those of Mr. Flight (known as Laycock's dairy) and of Messrs. Rhodes. Flight's is one of the curiosities of London; it covers fourteen acres of ground, surrounded by a high wall, and including buildings for the different purposes required. In the cow-house there are upward of 400 Cows, the whole of which are fed in stalls. The food is very properly varied; at one time they have mangel-wurzel; then they have turnips, carrots, cabbages, and clover; and, when fattening for market, they are fed on oil-cake and other articles. All are curried daily. Adjoining the cow-house is a hospital for unwell Cows, or Cows which are calving. The milk-house is kept beautifully clean, being scoured daily with hot water.

With respect to Rhodes's dairy, which is situated at Islington, Mr. Loudon, in his "Encyclopædia of Agriculture," has condensed the following description of its extent and mode of management from various publications:

"The number of Cows kept by the present Messrs. Rhodes exceeds, on an average of the year, four hundred: at one time these individuals are said to have had upward of a thousand Cows in their different establishments. The surface on which the buildings are placed is a slope of two or three acres, facing the east; and its inclination is about one inch in six feet. The sheds run in the direction of the slope—as well for the natural drainage of the gutters, and the more easily scraping, sweeping, and wheeling out of the manure, as for supplying water for drinking to small cast-iron troughs, which are fixed in the walls, at the heads of the cattle, in such a manner as that the one trough may be supplied from the other throughout the whole length of the shed. The sheds are twenty-four feet wide; the side walls about eight feet high; the roof of tiles, with rising shutters for ventilation, and with panes of glass, glazed into cast-iron skeleton tiles, for light. The floor is nearly flat, with a gutter along the center; and a row of stalls, each seven feet and a half wide, and adapted for two Cows, runs along the sides. The Cows are fastened by chains and rings, which rings run on upright iron rods, in the corners of the stalls—the common mode being departed from only in having iron rods instead of wooden posts. A trough or manger, formed of stone, slate, or cement, of the ordinary size of those used for horses, and with its upper surface about eighteen inches from the ground, is fixed at the head of each stall. Four sheds are placed parallel and close to each other, and in the party walls are openings, about a foot in breadth and four feet high, opposite each Cow. The bottom of these openings is about nine inches higher than the upper surface of the troughs, and is formed by the upper surface of the one-foot-square cast-iron cisterns, which contain the water for drinking. Each cistern serves two Cows, which, of course, are in different sheds, but adjoining and opposite each other. All these troughs are supplied from one large cistern by pipes, in a manner which can be so readily conceived that we shall not stop to offer a description. Each of these troughs has a wooden cover, which is put on during the time the Cows are eating their grains, to prevent their drinking at the same time, and dropping grains in the water. At the upper end, and at one corner of this quadruple range of sheds, is the dairy, which consists of three rooms of about twelve feet square: the outer or measuring room; the middle or scalding room, with a fire place and a boiler; and the inner or milk and butter-room, separated by a passage from the last. At the lower end of the range is a square yard, surrounded by sheds—one for fattening the Cows when they have ceased to give milk, and the others for store and breeding pigs. The pigs are kept for the purpose of consuming the casual stock of skim milk which occasionally remains on hand, owing to the fluctuations in the demand. This milk is kept in a well, walled with brick laid in cement, about six feet in diameter and twelve feet deep. The milk becomes sour there in a very short time, and, as is well known, is found most nourishing to the pigs when given in that state. Breeding swine are found most profitable, the sucking pigs being sold for roasting. Beyond this yard is a deep and wide pit or pond, into which the dung is emptied from a platform of boards projecting into it. The only remaining building wanted to complete the dairy establishment is a house or pit for containing the exhausted malt (grains), on which the Cows are chiefly fed. Messrs. Rhodes have a building or pit of this description at some distance, where they have a smaller establishment. There are a stack-yard, sheds, and pits for roots, straw, and hay, a place for cutting hay into chaff, cart-sheds, stables, a counting-house, and other buildings and places common to all such establishments, which it is not necessary to describe.

"The Cows in Rhodes's dairy are purchased newly calved in the cow-market held in Islington every Monday. They are kept as long as they continue to give not less than two gallons of milk a day, and are then fattened on oil-cake, grains, and cut clover hay, for the butcher. The Short-Horned breed is preferred, partly for the usual reason of being more abundant milkers than the Long-Horns, partly because the shortness of their horns allows them to be placed closer together, and partly because this breed is more frequently brought to market than any other. The Ayrshire breed has been tried to the number of 150 at a time, and highly approved of, as affording a very rich cream, as fattening in a very short time when they have left off giving milk, and as producing a beef which sold much higher than that of the Short-Horns. The difficulty, however, in procuring this breed was found so great that Mr. Rhodes was obliged to leave it off.—The length of time during which a Cow, treated as in this establishment, continues to give milk, varies from six months to the almost incredible period of two years. We were assured of there being at this moment several Cows among the 390 which we saw, that had stood in their places even more than two years, and continued to give upward of one gallon of milk daily.

"The treatment of the Cows in Rhodes's dairy differs from that in most other establishments. The Cows are never untied during the whole period that they remain in the house. In most other establishments, if not in all, stall-fed Cows or cattle are let out at least once a day to drink; but these animals have clear water continually before them. They are kept very clean, and the sheds are so remarkably well ventilated, by means of the openings in the roofs, that the air seemed to us purer than that of any cow-house we had ever before examined; probably from its direct perpendicular entrance through the roof—this, in moderate weather, being certainly far preferable to its horizontal entrance through the side walls.

"The principal food of the Cows in Rhodes's dairy, as in all the other London establishments, consists of grains—that is, malt after it has been used by the brewer or the distiller. As the brewing seasons are chiefly autumn and spring, a stock of grains is laid in at these seasons sufficient for the rest of the year.—The grains are generally laid in pits, bottomed and lined with brickwork set in cement, from ten to twenty feet deep, about twelve or sixteen feet wide, and of any convenient length. The grains are firmly trodden down by men—the heaps being finished like hayricks, or ridges in which potatoes are laid up for the winter, and covered with from six to nine inches of moist earth or mud, to keep out the rain and frost in winter and the heat in summer. As a Cow consumes about a bushel of grains a day, it is easy to calculate the quantity required to be laid in. The grains are warm, smoking, and in a state of fermentation, when put in, and they continue fit for use for several years—becoming somewhat sour, but they are, it is said, as much relished by the Cows as when fresh. It is common to keep grains two or three years; but in this establishment they have been kept nine years, and found perfectly good. The exclusion of the air almost prevents the increase of the fermentation and consequent decomposition. What is called distillers' wash—which is the remainder, after distillation, of a decoction of ground malt and meal—is also given to Cows, but more frequently to such as are fattening than to those in milk. The present price of brewers' grains is fourpence halfpenny per bushel; of distillers' grains, on account of the meal which they contain, ninepence a bushel; of wash, thirty-six gallons for sixpence.

"Salt is given to the Cows in Rhodes's dairy at the rate of two ounces each Cow a day. It is mixed with the grains, which are supplied before milking, about three o'clock in the morning; and in the afternoon, about two o'clock, just before milking. Of green food or roots, portions are supplied alternately with the grains; and in winter, when tares or green grass cannot be procured, after the turnips, potatoes, or mangel-wurzel have been eaten, a portion of dry hay is given.

"The produce of this dairy is almost entirely milk and cream for private families and for public hospitals and other institutions. A number of the public establishments are supplied directly from the dairy by contract; but private families are principally supplied by milk-dealers: these have what are called milk-walks—that is, a certain number of customers, whom they call upon with supplies twice a day; and they are thus enabled to ascertain the average of what their customers consume, and to contract with Messrs. Rhodes for this average. The latter calculate the number of Cows sufficient to give the dealer the supply wanted, and this number the dealer undertakes to milk twice a day—namely, at three o'clock in the morning, and at three in the afternoon. The milk is measured to the dealer, and should he have milked more than his quantity, it remains with the dairyman; but should the Cows have been deficient in the quantity, it is made good from the milk of other Cows, milked on account of the contracts of the establishment. As the supply of the Cows and the demand of the dealers are continually varying, it often happens that considerable quantities of milk remain on the dairyman's hands—frequently, we are told, as much as sixty or seventy gallons a day. This quantity is placed in shallow earthen vessels, to throw up the cream in the usual manner; this cream is churned, and the butter sold." The skimmed milk, it is added, as well as the buttermilk, are, as is usual in English dairies, given to the pigs.

NEW-YORK DAIRY MANAGEMENT.

In contrast to the above, we here insert some remarks more immediately applicable to the management of the New-York Dairies, from HARTLEY's ESSAY ON MILK, published in New-York in the year 1842:

"The manner of producing milk to supply the inhabitants of cities and other populous places is so contrary to our knowledge of the laws which govern the animal economy, that from a bare statement of the facts, any intelligent mind might confidently anticipate the evils which actually result from it. The natural and healthy condition of the Cows appears, for the most part, to be utterly disregarded. They are literally crowded together in large numbers in filthy pens, which at once deprives them of adequate exercise and pure air, both of which are indispensably essential to their health. Instead of being supplied with food suited to the masticatory and digestive organs of herbivorous and ruminant animals, they are most generally treated as if omnivorous; and their stomachs are gorged with any description of aliment, however unhealthy, which can be most easily and cheaply procured, and will produce the greatest quantity of milk. Thus, in the vicinities of the cities of New-York and Brooklyn, in America, and indeed wherever grain distilleries abound, either in this country or in Europe, *distillery-slop* is extensively used.* In London and other places where *brewers' grains* can be obtained, they are in great requisition for milk-dairies; while in grape-growing countries, the *refuse of the grape* is used for the same purpose, and with effects as pernicious as those produced by the dregs of the distillery. Besides these unhealthy aliments, in other cases decayed vegetables, and the sour and putrid offals and remnants of kitchens, are in populous places carefully gathered up as food for milch Cows. As might be expected, the cattle, under this most unnatural management, become diseased, and the lactescent secretions not only partake of the same nature, but are impure, unhealthy, and innutritious. Yet this milk is the chief aliment of children in all places where the population is condensed in great numbers; it is the nourishment chosen and relied upon to develop the physical powers and impart vigor to the constitution during the most feeble and critical period of human life, when the best possible nourishment is especially necessary in order to counteract the injurious effects of the infected air and deficient exercise, which are often inseparable from the conditions of a city life.

"So few are the exceptions to these modes of producing and using milk under the circumstances named, that they may be said to be nearly universal, both in this and in most other countries. And when it is recollected that in the United States about one-third of the population live in masses, and in Europe a vastly greater proportion, some adequate idea may be formed of the extent to which the evils consequent upon the use of an essential but an unhealthy article of food, prevail."

"But slop alone, as food for fattening cattle, is of little value. On such unnatural aliment they become diseased and emaciated. Cows plentifully supplied with it, may yield abundance of milk; but it is notorious that the article thus produced is so defective in the properties essential to good milk, that it cannot be converted into butter or cheese, of course is good for nothing—except to sell. But in country places milk cannot be turned to account in this way for there are no buyers, and as slop is not in request for stock or dairies, if the distiller would find the most advantageous market for it, he must conduct his operations in the vicinity of populous places. This, we repeat, is one among other reasons why such localities are desired. He finds it less profitable to fatten swine upon slop, on account of the risk of killing them to his own detriment, than to have it fed to human beings through the agency of the dairyman."

"It has been estimated, after careful inquiry, that about ten thousand Cows in the city of New-York and neighborhood, are most inhumanly condemned to subsist on the residuum or slush of this grain, after it has undergone a chemical

---

* Distillery-slop is the refuse of grain diffused through water after it has undergone a chemical change, the alcohol and farina being extracted by the processes of fermentation and distillation.

change, and reeking hot from the distilleries. This slush, moreover, after the ceremony of straining through the organs of sickly Cows, as before stated, and duly colored and diluted and medicated, is sold to the citizens at an annual expense of more than a million dollars. The amount of disease and death consequent upon the sale and use of this milk, is doubtless recorded in the books of final judgment, and will hereafter be revealed. But the fact which chiefly concerns the public is, that this milk has been, and, it is believed, is now, extensively injurious and fatal to health and life."   .   .   .

"The Cow is an herbivorous and a ruminating animal; pasturage, of course, or gramineous matter, is its natural and appropriate aliment.

"Reasoning *a priori* from the physical formation of the Cow, as it is a ruminating animal, it were easy to demonstrate that its digestive organs are peculiarly adapted, and were designed by Nature, for solid food; and, consequently, that distillery slop and food of that description is the most unnatural aliment which it can receive into its stomach.

"The digestive organs of the ruminant class, such as the Cow and sheep, are more complicated than those of any other animals. In the first place, they have cutting or incisor teeth which are admirably adapted for cropping grass or pasturage. The upper external portion of these teeth is convex, rising straight from the gum; while inward they have a concave surface, gradually diminishing in thickness, and terminating in a sharp edge which is covered with enamel, so as to produce and retain the sharpness necessary for separating herbaceous substances. They have also large *molares*, or grinding teeth, fitted for comminuting grassy fibres, or food which requires long and difficult mastication, in order that the nourishment may be extracted from it; and for this purpose we find the enamel, or harder portions of the teeth, distributed over and throughout their texture. Besides this, they have large *salivary glands*, for the purpose of moistening and lubricating the food preparatory to swallowing, and to aid in the second process of mastication, during which the food is reduced to a pultaceous state; while, in carnivorous animals, these glands are either wanting, or of a much smaller size."   .   .   .

"One of the most notorious of the overgrown metropolitan milk-establishments, or rather the largest collection of slop-dairies—for there are many proprietors—is situated in the western suburbs of the city, near the termination, and between Fifteenth and Sixteenth streets, in New-York. The area occupied by the concern includes the greater part of two squares, extending from below the Ninth Avenue to the Hudson River, probably a distance of one thousand feet.— During the winter season, about two thousand Cows are said to be kept on the premises, but in summer the number is considerably reduced. The food of the Cows, of course, is *slop*, which being drawn off into large tanks, elevated some ten or fifteen feet, is thence conducted in close, square wooden gutters, and distributed to the different cow-pens, where it is received into triangular troughs, rudely constructed by the junction of two boards. The range of the pens being interrupted by the intersection of the Tenth-avenue, the slop is conveyed by means of a gutter underground to the opposite side of the road, where it is received into a capacious reservoir, and thence conducted to the pens, which extend to the margin of the river. In the vicinity of Brooklyn there is a similar establishment, which contains about *seven hundred* Cows; and in the neighborhood of that city and of New-York there are numerous smaller concerns, where the cattle are fed in like manner, by receiving the slop smoking hot directly from the distilleries. In the far greater number of cases, however, the dairies are too far from the distilleries to be supplied in this way. The slop is therefore carted in vast quantities from the distilleries, in hogsheads, to the smaller milk establishments, which are numerously scattered in the suburbs and neighborhoods of the cities to the distance of several miles.*

* Since the above was written, the author revisited some of the slop-milk manufactories in New-York, Brooklyn, Williamsburgh, Bushwick, the Wallabout, and vicinities, for the purpose of information. He learned that, at some of the establishments in these places, an unusual mortality had recently occurred among the milch Cows. The fact itself was indisputable; but owing to the unwillingness, not to say incivility, of the persons who supposed it was their interest to conceal the truth, nothing very definite in relation to the nature and extent of the disease was obtained. Some of the distilleries, we observed, had been enlarged, and others were undergoing repairs, which, occasioning a temporary failure of slop, the dairymen were carting it across the East River from New-York, for the supply of their cattle. The slop concerns and distilleries, though somewhat improved in *appearance* since public attention had been directed to them,

"The daily average quantity of slop for a Cow is about a barrel of *thirty-two gallons*. At first we were incredulous as to the amount they learn to consume; but after many careful inquiries at many dairies, the fact is rendered certain.— Now it is evident that no Cow in *health* would eat such an enormous quantity of slop. By feeding on this unnatural and stimulating food, they are thrown into a state of disease, and for a short time will feed monstrously, and yield large quantities of bad milk." . . . .

"The cow-pens are rude, unsightly wooden buildings, varying from fifty to two hundred feet in length, and about thirty feet in breadth. They are very irregularly arranged, so as to cover the entire ground, excepting narrow avenues between; and appear to have been temporarily constructed, as the arrival of new dairies required enlargements for their accommodation. It is said they will contain about two thousand head of cattle; but this estimate, we would judge, is an exaggeration. The stalls are rented by the proprietor of the distilleries to the different cow owners, at from four to five dollars a year per each head of cattle, while the slop is furnished at nine cents a barrel.* Slop constituting both food and drink, water and hay or other solid or gramineous fodder, supply no part of the wants of these abused animals. The fluid element, indeed, appears not to be in request for purifying purposes. Fountains of pure water, extensive hayricks, capacious out-houses, and similar conveniences, which are ordinarily deemed so important for the feeding and watering so large a stock, are here dispensed with as unnecessary appendages to a city dairy.

"The interior of the pens corresponds with the general bad arrangement and repulsive appearance of the exterior. Most of the cattle stand in rows of from seven to ten across the building, head to head and tail to tail alternately. There is a passage in the rear for cleaning, and another in front which gives access to the heads of the cattle. The floor is gently inclined, but no litter is allowed.— The stalls are three feet wide, with a partition between each, and a ceiling about seven feet high overhead. But the chief and most inexcusable defects are the want of ventilation and cleanliness; though in the latter respect, since public attention has been called to their vile condition, they are somewhat improved.— There appears, however, no contrivance for washing the pens, or by which a circulation of air can be produced. To scent the effluvia, as it is diluted and diffused in the surrounding atmosphere, is sufficiently offensive, and the visitor will instinctively retire in dread of closer proximity. But to survey the premises round about, and merely to look into the pens, will but inadequately convey an idea of the disgusting reality. . . . The astonishment is that animal life, with all its wonderful recuperative energies, and power of accommodation to circumstances, can exist in so fetid an atmosphere." . . . .

"Such, then, as described, is the barbarous and unnatural treatment of this docile, inoffensive and unfortunate animal, that is destined to supply us with nutriment, both when living and dead, and which is one of the most valuable gifts of Providence to ungrateful men." . . . .

"Slop-milk is naturally very thin, and of a pale bluish color. In order to dis-

---

were still spoken of by the inhabitants in the neighborhoods as nuisances of so offensive a character as to prevent the improvement of property in their vicinity; while their present vile condition too truly indicated the nature of the evils they were continuing to inflict on more distant portions of the community. The most careful inquiries, however, failed to elicit any new information of interest; but we everywhere received the fullest confirmation of the facts and principles which are spread throughout this work.

In the course of the tour, we visited a large rum-distillery located in the immediate neighborhood of the South Ferry, Brooklyn. We were not disappointed in failing of admittance into the concern, for it is common to all these establishments, which are battening on the spoils of an injured community, to conceal, as far as possible, their operations from the public eye. It was, however, of little consequence, for there were other means of information at hand, and much that was open to observation. We were informed that from *seven hundred* to *one thousand* bushels of grain are daily converted into whisky at this distillery, the refuse of which would suffice to slop *two thousand Cows*; and that about *fifty* head of cattle, and from *five* to *seven hundred swine*, were fattening on the premises. No milch Cows are there kept; but we counted *eighty-seven carts* and *wagons*, containing an aggregate of *one hundred and twenty-nine hogsheads*, apparently waiting for slush. exclusive of numerous others which were going and returning from the premises. The hour of our visit (3 o'clock P.M.) was inopportune to witness the daily delivery of the slop. The greatest activity in the business is from 4 to 8 o'clock morning and evening, during which time an incessant stream of carts is seen issuing from the distillery, laden with slop for the supply of the neighboring dairies.

The quantity of milk required for the *daily* supply of the cities of New-York and Brooklyn, as near as can be ascertained, is about *fifteen thousand gallons*. This, at the average price of six cents per quart, amounts to *three thousand seven hundred and fifty dollars* per day, or, in round numbers, to *fifteen hundred thousand dollars* a year.

* The price of slop is not uniform, but is varied by the value of grain. It has been as low as 6¼ cents per barrel.

guise its bad qualities and render it salable, it is necessary to give it color and consistence. That it is often adulterated is proved by analysis, and the confessions of those who from principle have relinquished the practice. Starch, sugar, flour, plaster of Paris, chalk, eggs, annatto, etc. are used for this purpose; such substances being preferred, of course, which have the strongest affinity for the fluid, and will not readily precipitate.* These adulterations enable the vender to give the milk a proper consistence and a beautiful white color, so as to dilute the wretched slush with about an equal quantity of water, without detection."

GENERAL MANAGEMENT OF CATTLE

Fattening Cattle for Market.

The stall-feeding or soiling of cattle is considered to possess several advantages over feeding in the fields. In field-feeding, the animals waste a certain quantity of pasture by treading and lying upon it, and by dropping their dung—the grass which grows on the dung spots being ever after rejected; the animals also spend time in seeking for the herbage which suits their fancy, and much is allowed to go to seed untouched. In stall-feeding, the whole time is devoted to eating and ruminating, while no food is lost, and the animals are brought to a higher condition. Another important advantage of soiling is that it uses up the waste straw of a farm as litter, and thus furnishes a plentiful supply of that indispensable article, manure, for the fields. Some feeders tie up their cattle to the stall while preparing for market; but others permit them to roam about on a thick bed of straw in an enclosure in the farm-yard, with a shed to retire to for shelter—the feeding in this case being from racks. Unless for a period during the final process of fattening, the straw-yard method is reckoned the best for keeping the cattle in a healthy state, and consequently for producing beef of the finest kind.— The practice of feeding cattle for a considerable length of time, in darkened stalls, on oil-cake, carrots, mangel-wurzel, &c. produces, as is well known, a great deposition of fat, and swells the animals to a monstrous size. The beef, however, of such over-fed cattle is never fine. The fat with which it is loaded easily escapes in cooking, and leaves lean of an inferior quality. The best sign of good meat is its being *marbled*, or the fat and lean well mixed, when brought to the table; and this is not to be expected from beef fed in an unnatural condition.

The age at which cattle are fattened depends upon the manner in which they have been reared—upon the properties of the breed in regard to a propensity to fatten earlier or later in life—and on the circumstances of their being employed in breeding, in labor, for the dairy, or reared solely for the butcher. In the latter case, the most improved breeds are fit for the shambles when about three years old, and very few of any large breed are kept more than a year longer. As to Cows and working Oxen, the age of fattening must necessarily be more indefinite; in most instances, the latter are put up to feed after working three years, or in the seventh or eighth year of their age.

Rules for Selecting Cattle.

In selecting cattle for feeding, their qualities may be in some measure known by examining the hide, horns, &c. "It is well known that the grazier and the butcher judge of the aptitude that any animal has to fatten from the touch of the skin. When the hide feels soft and silky, it strongly indicates a tendency in the animal to take on meat; and it is evident that a fine and soft skin must be more pliable, and more easily stretched out to receive any extraordinary quantity of flesh, than a thick or tough one. At the same time thick hides are of great importance in various manufactures. Indeed, they are necessary in cold countries, where cattle are much exposed to the inclemency of the seasons; and, in the best breeds of Highland cattle, the skin is thick in proportion to their size, without being so tough as to be prejudicial to their capacity of fattening. It appears, from Columella's description of the best kind of Ox, that the advantage of

---

* The presence of flour, starch, etc. in milk may be detected by adding to the milk a solution of iodine in alcohol or by adding a little nitric acid to the milk, and then a few drops of a solution of iodine of potassium. Either of these tests communicates a blue color to milk or cream which contains arrow-root, rice-powder, flour, or any other substance of which starch is the constituent. [*Domestic Chemist*, p. 148.

a soft skin is not a new discovery, but was perfectly well known to the husbandmen of ancient Italy." These are the observations of Sir John Sinclair, who adds the following as a summary of good points to be attended to in choosing cattle: "They should be—1. Of a moderate size, unless where the food is of a nature peculiarly forcing; 2. Of a shape the most likely to yield profit to the farmer; 3. Of a docile disposition, without being deficient in spirit; 4. Hardy, and not liable to disease; 5. Easily maintained, and on food not of a costly nature; 6. Arriving soon at maturity; 7. Producing considerable quantities of milk; 8. Having flesh of an excellent quality; 9. Having a tendency to take on fat; 10. Having a valuable hide; and, lastly, Calculated (should it be judged necessary) for working." It is thought best to begin to break-in Oxen at three years old, and to give them full work at four.

With respect to judging of cattle by their horns and teeth, we offer the following observations by Mr. Hickey:

"The ordinary guide for ascertaining the precise age of cattle is the horn, which is also indicative of the breed; at three years old (this is laid down as a rule) the horns are perfectly smooth, after this a ring appears near the root, and annually afterward a new circle, so that, by adding two years to the first ring, the age is calculated; but it has been clearly shown that this is a very uncertain mode of judging; 'that the rings are only distinct in the Cow;' and that 'if a Heifer goes to the Bull when she is two years old, or a little before or after that time, there is an immediate change in the horn, and the first ring appears; so that a real three-year old would carry the mark of a four-year old.' 'In the Bull they are either not seen until five, or they cannot be traced at all;' nor in the Ox do they 'appear until he is five years old, and they are often confused;' besides, 'there is also an instrument called a rasp, which has been said to make many an arm ache a little before a large fair.' Without any delusive intentions, however, an ugly set in the horns of young cattle is often remedied by filing a little off the sides of the tips opposite to the direction which it is desired that the horns should take.

"Some men have an antipathy to horns altogether, and would even carry their dislike so far as to extirpate them from the brows of all their cattle; they can indulge their taste by paring off the tops of the horns when they first break through the skin. Perhaps it is not generally known that the larger the horn the thinner the skull.

"The age is indicated with unerring certainty by the teeth, to those who have judgment and experience, until the animal reaches the age of six or seven; until two years old, no teeth are cast; at that age, two new teeth are cut; at three, two more are cut; and, in the two succeeding years, two in each year; at five, the mouth is said to be full, though not completely so until six, because until that period the two corner teeth (the last in renewal) are not perfectly up. The front or *incisor* teeth are those considered, for a full-grown beast has altogether thirty-two teeth."

Method of Ascertaining the Weight of Cattle while Living.

"This is of the utmost utility for all those who are not experienced judges by the eye; and, by the following directions, the weight can be ascertained within a mere trifle:—Take a string, put it round the beast, standing square, just behind the shoulder-blade; measure on a foot-rule the feet and inches the animal is in circumference—this is called the girth; then, with the string, measure from the bone of the tail which plumbs the line with the hinder part of the buttock; direct the line along the back to the fore part of the shoulder-blade; take the dimensions on the foot-rule as before, which is the length, and work the figures in the following manner:—Girth of the bullock, 6 feet 4 inches; length, 5 feet 3 inches; which, multiplied together, make 31 square superficial feet; that again multiplied by 23 (the number of pounds allowed to each superficial foot of cattle measuring less than 7 and more than 5 in girth), makes 713 pounds; and, allowing 14 pounds to the stone, is 50 stone 13 pounds. Where the animal measures less than 9 and more than 7 feet in girth, 31 is the number of pounds to each superficial foot. Again, suppose a pig or any small beast should measure 2 feet in girth, and 2 feet along the back, which, multiplied together, make 4 square feet; that, multiplied by 11, the number of pounds allowed for each square foot of cattle measuring less than 3 feet in girth, makes 44 pounds; which, divided by 14, to bring it to stones, is 3 stone 2 pounds. Again, suppose a calf, a sheep, &c. should measure 4 feet 6 inches in girth, and 3 feet 9 inches in length, which, multiplied together, make 16¼ square feet; that multiplied by 16, the number of pounds allowed to all cattle measuring less than 5 feet, and more than 3 in girth, makes 264 pounds; which, divided by 14, to bring it into stones, is 18 stone 12 pounds. The dimensions of the girth and length of black cattle, sheep, calves, or hogs, may be as exactly taken this way as is at all necessary for any computation or valuation of stock, and will answer exactly to the four quarters, sinking the offal; and which every man, who can get even a bit of chalk, can easily perform. A deduction must be made for a half-fatted beast, of 1 stone in 20, from that of a fat one; and, for a Cow that has had calves, 1 stone must be allowed, and another for not being properly fat.

Diseases and their Treatment.

Cattle are subject to various diseases, the result of improper treatment or of causes connected with climate which it is difficult to avert. By attention to feeding, housing, and cleaning, much may be done to prevent some of the more fatal distempers. Cattle that have passed their lives, both day and night, in the open air, are generally so hardy that they are not injured by a wetting of the skin, and are liable to few of the complaints of dairy or stall-fed animals. Cows being compelled to lead an artificial mode of life, are the most delicate in every respect, and require the most careful treatment. They should not be left out all night; and, when they return from the field wet, it is always a safe and humane plan to dry them with a wisp of straw. The diseases to which they are most liable are of an inflammatory kind, and for these the veterinary surgeon prescribes bleeding, and perhaps some medicines to be taken internally.

Though it is by no means our design to offer, in this work on *Milch Cows*, any thing like a general work on cattle, it is deemed well enough, besides the general description of the breeds most in use, to give a few recipes for the most common diseases of *Cows and Calves*.

Of *Calves*, the maladies which most frequently occur are *diarrhœa*, and its opposite, *costiveness*. The common diarrhœa, or scouring, in Calves, arises generally from irregular feeding, or other bad management.

Nothing is more apt to disorder the bowels of the young Calf than the too common practice of attempting to substitute other diet for that of milk, or milk diet at an unnatural temperature. The young ruminant (says that high authority, C. W. Johnson), subsisting on the milk of its mother, does not require that complicated system of stomachs which afterward becomes necessary for the proper comminution of its food. Accordingly we find that the aperture of the first and second stomach is, in the Calf, entirely closed, and the folds of the third adhere together so as to form a narrow tube. The milk passes at once into the fourth stomach, which is the seat of true digestion. This arrangement of itself indicates that the food of the young animal ought to be liquid, even when it is deprived of the milk of its parent. It is for this reason that the weaning of the Calf must take place very gradually.

For SCOURING, the same author recommends the following as an excellent remedy: Prepared chalk, 4 ounces; Laudanum, 1 ounce;
Powdered canella bark, 1 ounce; Water, 1 pint.

Mix these together, and give two or three table-spoonsful, according to the size of the Calf, twice or three times a day.

COSTIVENESS IN CALVES.—For this complaint dissolve from two to four ounces, according to age, of Epsom salts in two quarts of water, and inject into the stomach by means of the stomach pump, and, in need, repeat in half doses every four hours.

CATARRH (common), or HOOSE (common cold).—This is a common complaint, much too often neglected till it degenerates into worse disorders.

For Cattle.—In slight cases house them, give them mashes, or a dose of physic. In more severe cases bleed, and after bleeding give—

Epsom salts, ½ pound, Powdered aniseed, 2 ounces;
Ginger, 2 drachms; Gruel, 3 pints.

For epidemic catarrh or influenza, bleed from three to five or six quarts, and give the following purging drench:

Epsom salts, 1 pound; Powdered coriander seeds, 1 ounce.
Dissolve in 3 pints of warm gruel.

THE COW AND THE DAIRY.   35

Should the fever continue after the purging drench, the following fever drench must be given night and morning:

Tartar emetic, 1 drachm;   Nitre, 4 drachms.

Mix and give in a quart of warm gruel.

CLEANSING.—The *after-birth* or placenta should be discharged soon after the period of calving; in case this is delayed, a dose of physic may be administered, composed of one pound of Epsom salts, and two drachms of ginger in some warm water or warm gruel. Leave the Calf with the Cow for some time after it is born.

The following cleansing drink may be given with advantage:

Cummin seed powder, 2 ounces;   Sulphur, 2 ounces;
Bay berries powdered, 1 ounce;   Turmeric, 1 ounce.

Boil these together for ten minutes, and give the drink when cool in some gruel.

CLYSTERS.—Clysters are medicines introduced (commonly by a syringe) into the rectum of animals. The composition of the most common is as follows:

Clyster for Cows.

Epsom salts, 1 pound;   Linseed oil, 8 ounces;   Water, 3 or 4 quarts.

Very useful to assist the operation of physic drenches.

CUD, LOSS OF—Is not a disease of itself, but is usually a symptom of various disorders. The following drink may be given in cases of loss of cud, when no indication of any particular disorder is apparent:

Epsom salts, ½ pound;   Carraway seeds, powdered, 1 ounce;
Gentian, powdered, ½ ounce;   Ginger, powdered, 2 drachms.

Mix, and give in warm gruel.

Rumination is requisite in order to keep an ox in health. A little straw or hay is accordingly necessary to enable it to chew the cud. We know a case in which barley-meal and boiled potatoes were given to Cows without hay or straw. Constipation resulted, and the cattle nearly perished from the ignorance of the feeder.

DIARRHŒA—Is the excessive discharge of fæcal matter. It arises from various causes, as from too much opening physic, poisonous plants, bad treatment, foul water, or from some peculiar state of the atmosphere. This may be treated as follows:—First give an aperient—either one pint of linseed oil, or, in a quart of water—

Epsom salts, ½ pound;   Powdered ginger, 2 drachms.   Mix for a dose.

Afterward give the following astringent:

Prepared chalk, 1 ounce;   Powdered opium, ½ drachm;
Powdered catechu, 3 drachms;   Powdered ginger, 2 drachms.

Mix, and give in a quart of warm gruel.

FLOODING—Is a discharge of blood from the uterus of the Cow, after calving. The only remedy is to apply cold to the loins: if in warm weather, a pound of saltpetre dissolved in a gallon of water will produce a very cold solution. If ice can be procured, equal parts of snow and ice, say equal parts of each, will produce a very intense cold. If the flooding still continues, raise the Cow's hind parts, give two drachms of opium every hour, keep the patient quiet, take away her Calf.

GARGET—Arises from the inflamed and hardened state of the internal substance of the udder of Cows. This is a complaint which is very apt to arise in young Cows. In the early stages of it, the best remedy is to allow her Calf to suckle, and rub about her udder. If this does not effect a cure, then it is generally necessary to take away a little blood, and afterward to give the following drench:

Epsom salts, 1 pound;   Aniseed powdered, 1 ounce;   Warm water, 3 pints.

The udder to be bathed with hot water three times a day, and after each bathing to be well rubbed with the following ointment:

Yellow basilicon, 4 ounces;   Camphor, 1 ounce, rubbed down with a little spirits of wine;
Strong mercurial ointment, 2 ounces;   Soft soap, 16 ounces.   Rub these well together.

In very obstinate cases I have found the following successful:

Hydriodate of potash, 1 drachm, rubbed into very fine powder and mixed with 1 ounce of spermaceti ointment.

After bathing with hot water, a piece of the size of a small nutmeg should be well rubbed in, night and morning.

KICKS, AND OTHER BRUISES.—Foment the parts copiously and frequently for some time with hot water; if the skin is broken, apply the following tincture:

Friar's balsam, 2 ounces;   Tincture of aloes and myrrh, 2 ounces.   Mix for use.

MISCARRIAGE.—The usual period of gestation in a Cow is two hundred and seventy days, or nine calendar months; but there is much variation in the time of the Cow being with calf. According to M. Tessier, in eleven hundred and thirty-one Cows upon which his observations were made, the shortest period was two hundred and forty, and the longest three hundred and twenty-one—being a variation of eighty-one days; or, reckoning from nine months, fifty-one days over, and thirty-one days under. Of five hundred and seventy-five Cows, he found twenty-one calved between the two hundred and fortieth and two hundred and seventieth day; five hundred and forty-four between the two hundred and seventieth and two hundred and ninety-ninth, and ten between the two hundred and ninety-ninth and three hundred and twenty-first day. It has been remarked that the Cow goes longer with a bull calf than with a cow calf. Of seven hundred and sixty-four Cows, noted by Lord Spencer *(Jour. Royal Agri. Soc.*, vol. i., p. 165), two hundred and twenty days was the shortest period when a *live* calf was produced, and two hundred and forty-two days the shortest period when the calf was *reared*; three hundred and thirteen days was the *longest* period he remarked a Cow to be in calf; three hundred and fourteen Cows calved before the two hundred and eighty-fourth day, and three hundred and ten after the two hundred and eighty-eighth day.

Miscarriage occurs oftener in the Cow than in all other domestic animals put together. Perhaps it is one of the greatest annoyances the proprietor of Cows has to encounter; and unfortunately, for aught we see to the contrary, it is likely so to continue; for, in spite of the improved state of veterinary medicine, and the researches of skillful veterinary surgeons, both at home and abroad, miscarriage still continues as frequent and annoying as ever. The causes are frequently involved in obscurity; but it may be mentioned that an extremely hot and foul cow-house, a severe blow, violent exertion, starvation, plethora, an overloaded stomach, internal inflammations, constipated bowels, bad food or water, improper exposure and the like, will now and then produce miscarriage. Anything whatever, indeed, that seriously affects the health of the animal in general, or the state of the reproductive organs in particular, may do so. But miscarriage occurs again and again when no such causes as those enumerated can be traced. The disease, if such it may be called —as I think it may—is even said to be infectious. No sooner does it show itself in one animal than it is seen in another, and another, till it has spread over the most part of the cow-house. Some say this is to be attributed to the odor arising from the substances evacuated. Possibly it may be so; there is nothing unreasonable in the supposition: for although we cannot perceive the smell, nor account for its peculiar influence, it is still quite within possibility that such an odor does exist, having the power attributed to it. There can be no great harm, however, in acting as if we were assured that the mischief has its origin in the source so commonly supposed, provided we do not shut our eyes to any other which accident or investigation may reveal. In the meantime, the number of miscarriages may be diminished by carefully avoiding all those causes which are known to be capable of producing it. Let the Cows be regularly fed; let their food be good and in proper quantities; let them have water as often as they will take it; avoid sudden exposure to cold or heat; and, above all, let the cow-house be well ventilated. Prohibit all manner of rough usage on the part of those who look after the Cows, whether they be pregnant or not. If any of them accumulate flesh too rapidly, gradually reduce their allowance; and, on the other hand, if any become emaciated, discover the cause, and remedy it, always by slow degrees. Sudden changes in the matter or mode of feeding should also be avoided. The same sort of diet does not agree equally well with all the Cows; and this, in general, is indicated by undue relaxation or constipation of the bowels: this should be watched, and removed at once. Attention to these and many other minor circumstances will amply repay the proprietor for the little additional trouble.

"When the farmer perceives symptoms of miscarriage, he should," says Professor Youatt, in his excellent work on Cattle, "remove the Cow from the pasture to a comfortable cow-house or shed. If the discharge is glairing, but not offensive, he may hope that the calf is not dead—he will be assured of this by the motion of the fœtus, and then it is impossible that the miscarriage may yet be avoided. He should hasten to bleed her, and that copiously, in proportion to her age, size, condition, and the state of excitement in which he may find her; and he should give a dose of physic immediately after the bleeding (this may be 1 lb. of Epsom salts in a quart of warm water). The physic beginning to operate, he should administer half a drachm of opium, and half an ounce of sweet spirits of nitre; unless she is in a state of great debility, he should avoid, above all things, the *comfortable drink* which some persons recommend; he should allow nothing but gruel, and keep his patient as quiet as he can. By these means he may occasionally allay the general or local irritation that precedes or causes the miscarriage, and the Cow may yet go her full time."

WOMB INFLAMMATION.—This affection of the womb occurs after calving or bulling. The symptoms are, great irritation and pain. Bleed and give the following drench:
Epsom salts, 1 pound; Powdered carraway seeds, 2 ounces; Warm gruel, 3 pints.
Bathe the womb with Goulard water, or vinegar and water in equal parts.

CALVING TABLE.

Day bulled.	Will calve.	Day bulled.	Will calve.	Day bulled.	Will calve.	Day bulled.	Will calve.
Jan. 1	Oct. 8	April 1	Jan. 6	July 1	April 7	Oct. 1	July 9
" 7	" 14	" 7	" 12	" 7	" 13	" 7	" 15
" 14	" 21	" 14	" 19	" 14	" 20	" 14	" 22
" 21	" 28	" 21	" 26	" 21	" 28	" 21	" 22
" 28	Nov. 4	" 28	Feb. 2	" 28	May 4	" 28	Aug. 5
" 31	" 7	" 30	" 4	" 31	" 8	" 31	" 8
Feb. 1	" 8	May 1	" 5	Aug. 1	" 9	Nov. 1	" 9
" 7	" 14	" 7	" 11	" 7	" 15	" 7	" 15
" 14	" 21	" 14	" 18	" 14	" 22	" 14	" 21
" 21	" 28	" 21	" 25	" 21	" 29	" 21	" 29
" 28	Dec. 5	" 28	Mar. 4	" 28	June 5	" 28	Sept. 5
Mar. 1	" 6	" 31	" 7	" 31	" 8	" 30	" 7
" 7	" 12	June 1	" 8	Sept. 1	" 9	Dec. 1	" 8
" 14	" 19	" 7	" 14	" 7	" 15	" 7	" 21
" 21	" 26	" 14	" 21	" 14	" 22	" 14	" 21
" 28	Jan. 2	" 21	" 28	" 21	" 29	" 21	" 28
" 31	" 5	" 28	April 4	" 28	July 6	" 28	Oct. 5
		" 30	" 6	" 30	" 8	" 31	" 8

THE SPAYING OF COWS.

TRANSLATED FOR THE WORKING FARMER,

FROM "LA NORMANDIE AGRICOLE JOURNAL D'AGRICULTURE PRATIQUE," &c., &c.

STATEMENT OF M. P. A. MORIN, VETERINARY SURGEON AT THE ROYAL DEPOT AT LANGONNET.

A LAND owner in the United States, Mr. Winn, seems to have had the first practice in spaying cows. The object of the operation was to maintain in the cow, without interruption, a supply of the same quantity of milk that she gave at the time of spaying. Notwithstanding the favorable results that Mr. Winn claimed to have obtained, the operation remained almost unknown in France until a veterinary surgeon of Lausanne (a Swiss), M. Levrat made known the experiments practised by him, and their effects. The *Treatise of M. Levrat* ends with the following conclusions:—

"The effect of spaying seems to me to cause *a more abundant and constant secretion of milk*, which possesses also *superior qualities*, whence the following advantages result to the proprietor:

"1. An increase of one third in the quantity of milk.

"2. The certainty of having almost constantly the same quantity of milk.

"3. Exemption from accidents which may happen during the period of heat, when the cows mount each other, or are covered by too large bulls.

"4. Exemption from the risk of accidents which sometimes accompany or follow gestation and calving.

"5. Ease in fatting cows, when their milk begins to dry up.

"6. In fine, spaying is the only means of preventing onerous expenses, occasioned by cows becoming 'taurelieres,' which is so frequently the case in some countries, that it is rare to see cows kept more than two or three years without getting in this state: as for example, in the environs of Lausanne and Lavaux, where they are obliged for this reason to change all their cows every two or three years, which is quite ruinous."

M. Levrat confirmed, after a year's observations, this fact, that the quantity of milk was constantly kept the same after the time of spaying.

M. Régère, veterinary surgeon at Bordeaux, inserted in the *Recuel de Médecine Vétérinaire*, a series of facts upon the spaying of cows, that had been acted upon by various proprietors.

It appears from these facts, which he recounts with many details, and whose authenticity is fixed, that the spayed cows have given without interruption after the operation, a quantity of milk at least double the average of what they gave during the preceding years. "After the researches that I have made since I commenced all these experiments, to the present time," says M. Régère, "this calculation is very exact, and if the cows continue to give milk during their whole life, in like manner, the operation of spaying will furnish incontestable advantages, particularly in large cities, and their vicinity, where fodder is very dear, and where milk always sells well."

A remark made by MM. Levret and Régère, is that some cows, although they have been spayed, have had their heat, notwithstanding the removal of their ovarium, and the incapacity for their reproduction. These animals present, at the time of their heat, this difference from what we remark during the same period in cows not spayed, that their milk does not undergo any alteration in either quantity or quality.

We may add, that the school of Alfort has, recently, practised this operation upon different cows, and that all the results obtained have reached the point we have above stated.

Leaving this, we arrive at the facts determined by M. Morin.

"Young cows ought to receive that nourishment which favors the secretion of milk, and which in consequence renders active their lactiferous vessels. The cow is not usually in full production until after the third or fourth calf; she continues to give the same return up to the seventh or eighth; from this time lactation diminishes after each new calving. On the other hand, from the moment that the cow has received the bull, and gradually as gestation advances, the quantity of milk progressively diminishes in most breeds, until three or four months before healthy parturition, the secretion of milk is almost nothing. It is to guard against this loss, and other inconveniences, that we lay down what we have obtained after some years' experience in spaying the cow, and the happy results that we meet with daily.

OF THE SPAYING OF THE COW AND THE ADVANTAGES OF THIS OPERATION.

"The operation of spaying in the cow is productive of great advantages.

"1. The cow spayed a short time after calving, that is to say, thirty or forty days afterward, and at the time when she gives the largest quantity of milk, continues to give the like quantity, if not during her whole lifetime, at least during many years, and at the time when the milk begins to dry up the animal fattens. We are able to add, moreover, at this day, certain facts, the result of many years' experiment, that the milk of the spayed cow, although as abundant, and sometimes more so, than before the operation, is of a superior quality to that from a cow not spayed; that it is uniform in its character, that it is richer, consequently more buttery, and that the butter is always of a golden color.

"We believe that we ought to remark in passing, that if we feed the spayed cow too abundantly, lactation diminishes, and that the beast promptly fattens. It is therefore important that the feeding should not be more than sufficient to enable us to obtain the desired result.

"2. The spayed cow fattens more easily; its flesh, age considered, is better than that of the ox; it is more tender and more juicy.

"Indeed, no one is ignorant of the fact that all domestic animals, females as well as males, deprived of their procreative organs, fatten more quickly than those which retain them; that the flesh of the spayed females is more tender and more delicate than that of males. The same phenomena take place among spayed cows that occur among other females that have submitted to this operation; so, besides the advantage of furnishing a long-continued supply, before commencing a course of fattening, of abundant milk, and butter of a superior quality, the cow fattens easily and completely, and a certain benefit follows this course.

"3. In spaying decrepit cows, that is to say; of the age of from six to seven years, puny, small ones; those which, though fine in appearance bear badly; those which are subject to miscarriage; those which frequently experience difficult calving, or delivery; those difficult to keep; and finally, all those that are *taurelieres*, that is to say, constantly in heat—we have in addition to an abundant production of milk and butter, and a facility of fattening, the advantage of preventing a degeneration of the species, and moreover of avoiding a crowd of accidents or maladies which frequently take place during or after gestation, and of diminishing those which happen during the period of heat, such as that of heavy cows mounting others, or being jumped upon by too heavy bulls.

"Except under peculiar circumstances, we should take care in spaying the cow, that its teats have acquired their complete development, and that the milk has the proper qualities. The most suitable time is after the third or fourth calving.

"Many societies of agriculture, impressed with the important results that this operation effects, fix yearly at their agricultural meetings, premiums for the encouragement of the spaying of old cows. We doubt not that other societies who have not yet adopted this plan—not being convinced of its importance—when they are, will imitate their example. By this means they bestow upon the country a new source of products.

"We have been engaged for four years in researches upon this valuable discovery, we believe that it is incumbent upon us to state the results that we have obtained up to the present time. In the number of twenty-seven cows, aged from six to fifteen years, that we have actually spayed, we have had the following results: 1. Increase of milk in cows of six years; 2. Constant production in those that have passed that age; 3. Milk richer than that of the cow not spayed, consequently more buttery, and the butter both of a uniformly golden color, and having an aroma and taste far superior to that of a cow that has not undergone this operation.

"Early in July, 1842, we obtained as a subject of experiment, a cow from Brittany, of the small kind, twelve years old, calved about two months before, and which gave when we obtained her, about six quarts of milk daily. The next day after we performed the operation of spaying, indeed the first eight days after that, the secretion of milk sensibly diminished, in consequence of the light diet on which she had been put; but, on the ninth day, the time at which the cure was complete and the cow put on her ordinary food, the milk promptly returned as to its former quantity, and she at the same time assumed a plumpness that she had not had previously. Customarily bringing together, the yield of three days for butter-making being eighteen quarts, it produced constantly two kilograms of butter of the best quality. From the month of December to the following March, the quantity of milk diminished about one third, and the butter proportionally, the cow during that time having been put on dry fodder. But so soon as we were able to turn her into pasture—about the beginning of April—the milk, after eight days of this new food, resumed its former course, and the animal continued daily to furnish the same relative amounts of milk and butter as before.

"Three cows, two of which were fourteen years old, and the other fifteen, have dried up two years after the operation, and at the same time promptly fattened, without increase or change of food.

"One cow eight years old, plentifully supplied with trefoil and cabbage, gave, a short time after the operation, a quantity of milk nearly double that which she gave before, although she was kept on the same kind of food. She has during a year continued to furnish the same amount, and has in addition fattened so rapidly, that the owner has been obliged, seeing her fatness, to sell her to the butcher, although she was still very good for milk.

"Another fact, no less worthy of remark, we must not pass over in silence; and which goes to prove the superior and unchanging quality of the milk of a spayed cow. It is, that a proprietor having spayed a cow five years old, recently calved, with the special intention of feeding with her milk a newly-born infant, the infant arriving at the age of six months, of a robust constitution, refused its pap since it had been accidentally prepared with milk different from that of the spayed cow.

"The other cows which had been spayed continued to give entire satisfaction to their owners, as well in respect to the quantity and quality of the milk, as also by their good condition.

"Six cows manifested, shortly after the operation, and on divers occasions, the desire for copulation; but we have not remarked this peculiarity except among the younger ones. In other respects, as my colleagues, MM. Levrat and Régère, have stated, the milk has not indicated the least alteration in quantity or quality.

"Indeed, the happy results that are daily attained from this important discovery, are so conclusive, and so well known at this time in our part of the country, that as we write, many proprietors bring

THE SPAYING OF COWS. 39

us constantly good milch cows, since we have called upon them to do so, for us to practice the operation of spaying upon them. Every owner of cattle is aware, that from the time that the cow has received a bull, and in proportion as gestation advances, the milk changes and diminishes progressively, until at last, two or three months before a healthy parturition, the animal gives very little or no milk, whence ensues considerable loss; while at the same time, after the cows are subjected to the bull, the milk and butter are—for fifty days, at least—of a bad quality, and improper to be exposed for sale; but in addition to this, breeding cows are generally subjected to such loss in winter, and their keepers find themselves during a great part of the year, entirely deprived of milk and butter. and at a time, too, when they most need them.

"By causing the cows to undergo this operation, as we have mentioned in the preceding chapter, the owner will never fail of having milk and butter of excellent quality; will fatten his animals easily when they dry up, and also will improve the race, an anxiety for which is perceived in many provinces of France.

"In general, the means employed by farmers to obtain the best possible price for old cows, beyond being useful, or to use a commercial term, not merchantable, as to bring them to the bull, intending that gestation shall give them more suitable plumpness, so that they may be sold on more advantageous terms to the butcher; but does this state of fictitious *embonpoint* or fatness, render the flesh of these beasts better? Assuredly not. It is merely bloated, flabby flesh, livid, and which easily taints. Broth made from it is not rich, is without flavor, and without an agreeable smell; the lean and fat are in a measure infiltrated with water. and are consequently of bad quality and difficult sale. These causes ought then to determine farmers to adopt the advice we give; they, as well as the butcher and the consumer, will derive very great advantage from it.

"As our method of operating may be slightly different from that pointed out by our colleague, M. Levrat, we will describe that which we practice.

"Having covered the eyes of the cow to be operated upon. we place her against a wall, provided with five rings firmly fastened, and placed as follows: the first corresponds to the top of the withers; the second to the lower anterior part of the breast; the third is placed a little distance from the angle of the shoulder; the fourth is opposite to the anterior and superior part of the lower region, and the fifth, which is behind, answers to the under part of the buttocks. We place a strong assistant between the wall and the head of the animal, who firmly holds the left horn in his left hand, and with his right, the muzzle, which he elevates a little. This done, we pass through and fasten the end of a long and strong plaited cord in the ring, which corresponds to the lower part of the breast; we bring the free end of the cord along the left flank and pass it through the ring which is below and in front of the withers. We bring it down along the breast behind the shoulders and the angle of the fore leg to pass it through the third ring; from there, we pass it through the ring, which is at the top of the back; then it must be passed around against the outer angle of the left hip, and we fasten it, after having drawn it tightly to the posterior ring by a simple bow-knot.

"The cow being firmly fixed to the wall, we placed a cord, fastened by a slip-noose around its hocks to keep them together in such manner that the animal can not kick the operator, the free end of the cord and the tail are held by an assistant. The cow, thus secured, can not. during the operation, move forward. nor lie down, and the veterinary surgeon has all the ease desirable, and is protected from accident.

"M. Levrat advises that an assistant should hold a plank or bar of wood obliquely under the teats and before its limbs to ward off the kicks; but this method is not always without danger, both to the operator and the animal, because, at the commencement, that is, when the surgeon makes the incision through the hide and the muscles, the cow makes such sudden movements and tries so frequently to strike with its left hind foot, that it may happen that upon every movement, the plank or the bar may be struck against the operator's legs. On the other hand. although the defense may be firmly held by the assistant, yet it may happen, that in spite of his exertions, he sometimes may be thrown against the operator by the movements she may attempt, and there may be an uncontrollable displacement of the plank or bar; and then it may happen that she becomes wounded, and at the same time prevents the operation, while, by the mode we point out, there is no fear of accident, either to the operator or the beast. In case of the want of a wall provided with rings, we may use a strong palisade, a. solid fence, or two trees a suitable distance apart, across which we fix two strong bars of wood, separated from each other, according to the size of the cow.

"There is another means of confining them that we have employed for some time past, where the cows were very strong and irritable, more simple than the preceding, less fatiguing for the animal, less troublesome to the operator, and which answers perfectly. It consists: *First*. In leaving the cow almost free, covering her eyes, holding her head by two strong assistants, one of whom seizes the nose with his hand and strongly pinches the nostrils, whenever the animal makes any violent movements during the operation. *Second*. To cause another assistant to hold the two hind legs, kept together by means of a cord passed above and beneath the hocks; this assistant also holds the tail and pulls it, whenever the animal seeks to change its place.

"The cow being conveniently disposed, and the instruments and appliances, such as curved scissors upon a table, a convex edged bistoury, a straight one, and one buttoned at the point. suture needle filled with double thread of desired length, pledgets of lint of appropriate size and length, a mass of tow (in pledgets) being collected in a shallow basket. held by an intelligent assistant, we place ourselves opposite to the left flank, our back turned a little toward the head of the animal; we cut off the hair which covers the hide in the middle of the flanks, at an equal distance between the back and the hip, for the space of thirteen or fourteen centimetres in circumference; this done, we take the convex bistoury, and place it opened between our teeth. the edge out. the joint to the left; then, with both hands, we seize the hide in the middle of the flank and form of it a wrinkle of the requisite elevation, and running lengthwise of the body. We then direct an assistant to seize with his right hand the right side of this wrinkle; we then take the bistoury that we held in our teeth, and we cut the wrinkle at one stroke through the middle; the wrinkle having been suffered to go down, a separation of the hide is presented of sufficient length to enable us to introduce the hand; thereupon we separate the edges of the hide with the thumb and forefinger of the left hand, and in like manner, we cut through the abdominal muscles, the *iliax* (slightly obliquely) and the *lumbar* (across) for the distance of a centimetre from the lower extremity of the incision made in the hide; this done, armed with the straight bistoury, we make a puncture of the peritoneum at the upper extremity of the wound; we then introduce the buttoned bistoury, and move it obliquely from above to the lower part, up to the termination of the incision made in the abdominal muscles. The flank being opened, we introduce the right hand into the abdomen and direct it along the right side of the cavity of the pelvis, behind the *cul de saurumen* (paunch) and underneath the rectum, where we find the *cornes de l'uterus* (matrix); after we have ascertained the position of these viscera, we search for the *ovaires* (organs of reproduction), which are at the extremity of the *cornes*, and when we have found them, we seize them between the thumb and forefinger, detach them completely from the ligaments that keep them in their place, pull lightly, separating the cord, and the vessels (uterine or fallopian tube) at their place of union with the ovarium, by means of the nail of the thumb and forefinger, which presents itself at the point of touch; in fact we break the cord and bring away the ovarium. We then introduce again the hand in the abdominal cavity, and we proceed in the same manner to extract the other ovaria. This operation terminated, we, by the assistance of the needle, place a suture of three or four double threads waxed at an equal distance, and at two centimetres, or a little less from the lips of the wound, passing it through the divided tissues, we move from the left hand with the piece of thread; having reached that point, we fasten with a double knot, we place the seam in the intervals of the thread from the right, and as we approach the lips of the wound, we fasten by a simple knot, with a bow, being careful not to close too tightly the lower part of the seam, so that the suppuration which may be established in the wound, may be able to escape. This operation effected, we cover up the wound with a pledget of lint kept in its place by three or four threads passed through the stitches, and all is completed, and the cow is then led back to the stable.

"It happens, sometimes, that in cutting the muscles, of which we have before spoken, we cut one or two of the arteries which bleed so much, that there is necessity for a ligature before opening the peritoneal sac, because, if this precaution be omitted, blood will escape into the abdomen, and may occasion the most serious consequences.

CARE AFTER THE OPERATION.

The regimen that we prescribe during the first eight days following the operation, is a light diet, and a soothing lukewarm draught; if the weather should be cold, we cover the cow with a woollen covering. We must prevent the animal from licking the wound and from rubbing it against other bodies. The third day after the operation, we bathe morning and evening about the wound, with water of mallows lukewarm, and in default of this, we anoint it with a salve of hog's lard, and we administer an emollient glyster during three or four days.

"Eight days after the operation we take away the bandage, the lint, the fastenings and the threads; the wound is at that time completely cicatrized, as we have observed that a reunion takes place almost always by the first intention, as we have only observed suppuration in three cows, and then it was very slight. In this case we must use a slight pressure above the part where the suppuration is established, so as to cause the pus to leave it, and if it continues more than five or six days, we must supply emollients by alcolized water, or chloridized, especially if it be in summer. We then bring the cow gradually back to her ordinary nourishment.

"We have remarked in some cows a swelling of the body a short time after being spayed, a state that we have attributed to the introduction of cold air into the abdomen during the operation; but this derangement has generally ceased within twenty-four hours. If the contrary should occur, we administer one or two sudorific draughts; such as wine, warm cider, or a half glass of brandy, in a quart of warm water; treatment which suffices in a short time to re-establish a healthy state of the belly, the animal at the same time being protected by two coverings of wool.

"The operation which we have been describing, ought to be performed as we have said before, thirty to forty days after calving, upon a cow which has had her third or fourth calf, so that we may have a greater abundance of milk. The only precaution to be observed before the operation, is, that on the preceding evening we should not give so copious a meal as usual, and to operate in the morning before the animal has fed, so that the operator shall not find any obstacle from the primary digestive organs, especially the paunch, which, during its state of ordinary fullness, might prevent operating with facility.

CONCLUSION.

"From what has preceded, it is fixed and irrefutable,—1. That spaying induces permanency of milk, increase of quantity, and improvement of quality; richer, more buttery, superior color, finer taste and flavor. 2. The most suitable age is six years, and after the third or fourth calf. 3. The spayed cow fattens more easily, and furnishes beef of a better quality. 4. Cows that are bad breeders may be kept as good milkers, and the quality of good cattle kept up."

TREATISE.

ON

MILCH COWS:

WHEREBY

THE QUALITY AND QUANTITY OF MILK WHICH ANY COW WILL GIVE MAY BE ACCURATELY DETERMINED,

BY

OBSERVING NATURAL MARKS, OR EXTERNAL INDICATIONS ALONE;

THE LENGTH OF TIME SHE WILL CONTINUE TO GIVE MILK, &c. &c.

By M. FRANCIS GUENON, France.

Translated from the French of the Author, for the Farmers' Library,

By N. P. TRIST, late U. S. Consul at Havana.

THE TRANSLATOR TO THE READER.

Nonsense! Who can believe any such thing? What! by merely looking at a cow, to be able to tell how much milk she is capable of being made to yield; and, also, how long she can continue to give milk after being got with calf!—to be able thus to ascertain, not only what are the qualities of a full grown cow, but what are to be the qualities of any heifer-calf, by looking at her while yet but two or three months old! Surely, if ever there was a humbug, this is one.

Softly, Mr. Reader! You are very incredulous, no doubt, but I defy you to be more so than I was when in your present position. What is more, I defy you to cling to your skepticism over an hour or so. However strong and firm it may be at this moment, it will, in a little while, have vanished into nothing; and its place will be filled by another solid proof in addition to the many you must already have stored up, that

"There are more things in heaven and earth ——,
Than are dreamt of in your philosophy."

When this discovery was first mentioned to me, as one which had recently been published in France, I smiled at the credulity of some people. My informant, perceiving what effect the announcement had upon me, said, "It is so, however;" and then, nothing but politeness toward a stranger, for the first time under my roof, prevented my replying, "You do not really believe this to be possible."

He offered to send me the book; and, though I had not the least idea of throwing away my time in reading it, civility would not allow me to decline. It came, and I opened it with the intention merely of looking into it sufficiently to say that I had done so. When, however, in turning the pages over, I saw that this piece of quackery, as I felt very sure the pretended discovery must be, had engaged the attention of distinguished Agricultural Societies in France, and had earned "Gold Medals" for its author, in a country where they are not prone to be lavish of such substantial marks of approbation, my curiosity was awakened, and I had soon read enough to bring home to me once more, for the thousandth time, that homely old truth, "We live to learn."

Since then, many things have occurred to strengthen my confidence in the reality of this discovery, and in its high practical value to all interested in the preservation and improvement of milk stock—and who is it that is not interested in its productiveness? The most recent of these incidents is as follows:

A friend to whom I had lent the translation accompanied with the plates which are requisite to make it intelligible, showed it to a man from the country whose calling had rendered him quite conversant with the subject of cattle. This person's curiosity was so far awakened, that, beside attending to the explanations made to him, he took a sketch of some of the *escutcheons.* After an absence of some weeks, he returned to the city where this had happened, and came to see my friend. "That thing (said he) is as true as a book. There is no mistake about the matter. Since I was here, I have looked at more cows than ever you saw, and I am perfectly satisfied that the thing is just as the Frenchman says. I have become convinced, too, of another thing: that our breeds of cattle are by no means the great things they are cracked up to be."   N. P. T.

Washington City, January, 1846.

TREATISE ON MILCH COWS.

CHAPTER I.

ACCOUNT OF THE DISCOVERY.

To give the history of my discovery, I must speak of myself. My narrative shall be succinct and short, although my labors have been protracted. But this is a condition attached to discoveries generally; we must meditate long upon what an instant has sufficed to reveal or suggest to us. It will be seen that, in my case, difficulties were always renewing.

I am the son of a gardener, and I followed for a long time this trade of my forefathers. Nature had given me an observing turn of mind; I was fond of bringing things together—of instituting comparisons between them—of deducing consequences. At an early period I became possessed by the idea that I was destined to make some important discovery in the branch of industry which I followed. Was this the suggestion of mere vanity? Be it as it may, the thought took root in my mind, and became for me a fixed idea. With a view to arriving at this wished-for discovery, I studied the works of the best writers on Botany and Agriculture; I learned Geometry and the art of Drawing, so far as it seemed necessary to me. I followed up all the ramifications of the vegetable kingdom, and applied myself to the study of the external signs by which plants and vegetables of different sorts might be distinguished, and their qualities and productiveness might be known beforehand.

To do this was to accomplish a good deal, no doubt; but my mind, still possessed by the idea of the great future discovery, was never at rest. I was, like Ahasuerus, under the hand of the angel; a voice within was constantly crying out, "Go on!" and I felt myself impelled forward; but I had no glimpse of the goal to which I was tending.

Chance led to the discovery of the famous Tyrian purple; to chance also is due an observation which was the germ of my discovery, and constitutes the basis of my method. When fourteen years of age, I used, according to country custom, to drive our only Cow to the grazing ground. I was very fond of her, and could have identified her among ever so many. One day, as I was whiling away the time in cleaning and scratching my poor old companion, I noticed that a sort of bran or dandruf detached itself in considerable quantities from certain spots on her hind parts, formed by the meeting of the hair, as it grew in opposite directions; which spots I have since called *ears*, from the resemblance they often bear to the bearded ears or heads of wheat or rye.* This fact attracted my attention, and I recollected having heard one of my grandfathers say that it was probable there were external marks on Cows, whereby their good qualities or their defects might be known—just as we judge of the vital force of a plant and its qualities by means of its leaves and the lines on its skin. My own thoughts now took this turn. Reflecting on the subject, I arrived at the conclusion that if, in the vegetable kingdom, there exist external signs, whereby the good and the bad qualities of a plant can be positively known, there ought to exist in the animal kingdom, also, marks whereby we may judge, by inspecting an animal, of its qualities, good and bad; and I thought that I had discovered one of these signs.

All this, however, was as yet but mere speculation—a brilliant theory, which experience might belie: it was necessary to interrogate Nature. The Cow which I tended was a good milker. I have already said that I knew her perfectly. I examined other Cows within my reach, to see if I should find the same signs in them. I sought for the bearded *ears* (*quirls*), and scratched those spots in quest of dandruf; the abundance or the scarcity of this being what first engaged my attention. Every new Cow was compared with my own as a standard, and her superiority, equality or inferiority determined in my own mind.

From this moment I spared nothing to follow up my observations; no fatigue was too great for me; I have often traveled several leagues in order to examine a single Cow. What was my exultation when, after I had formed my judgment of a Cow, the questions with which I belabored her owner brought forth answers that corroborated its accuracy! How often has it happened that people were convinced that the animal whose qualities I was pronouncing upon must have been previously known to me! My secret was the cause of astonishment to many; I took good care to keep it to myself.

In the course of the comparisons thus instituted by me, with reference to the dandruf alone, which was at first the only thing that governed me, I had occasion to remark that great diversities existed among Cows, in respect to the shape of the bearded ears (*quirls*) which produced the dandruf. This suggested a new train of reflections and observations, which resulted in my becoming convinced that these *shapes* were the signs by which to distinguish Cows, and to know the good and bad qualities of every individual among them. From that moment my discovery was made; but it was necessary to digest it into a system—above all, to establish its accuracy in all its parts, by proofs which should carry my own conviction into the minds of others. It was here that all my courage and perseverance was put in requisition.

It did not suffice to have discovered signs that were characteristic of different sorts of Cows; it was necessary to make sure that the same mark might always be relied upon as a positive and certain sign of the same perfection or defect.—

---

* These marks are, in some parts of our country, called *quirls*. Their occurrence in horses (particularly on the neck, under the mane) is well known to be a sign of *blood*. This is a remarkable coincidence; and it seems far from improbable that the discovery made by the author in regard to neat cattle will lead to similar discoveries respecting other domestic animals. [*American Translator.*

This could not be effected except by studying a vast number of individuals—by comparing them together—taking into consideration the countries from which they came—their stature—their yield. This was not all: they had to be classed. Conceive what toil this task involved for me, a plain child of Nature, who had no idea of such a classification, and found myself under the necessity of establishing one. The endeavor was one to absorb me entirely; I gave up my calling; I traveled about, visiting cattle markets, fairs, cow-stables; I questioned and cross-questioned all who might be expected to know most on the subject—husbandmen, dealers in cattle, men of the veterinary profession; I became convinced that my discovery had not been anticipated by any one. The marks for distinguishing a good Cow from a bad one varied according to the notions of each individual. Some looked to the shape of the horns—others upon that of the udder; some judged by the shape of the animal, or the color of her hair—others were determined in their choice by something else. But, in these various modes of judging, all was vague and uncertain. I became confirmed in the belief that I had made the important discovery of signs that were positive and certain; and, in order the better to satisfy myself of the solidity of the ground upon which my method was to rest, I took the precaution to return to the same localities at different times and seasons, that I might trace and ascertain the effects which might attend these variations of Nature. All my observations were accurately noted down; and I could at length flatter myself with having acquired a mass of facts which gave solidity and consistence to my system, and imparted the character of positive certainty to that which at first had been but a probable conjecture.

In 1822, I began to deal in cattle on my own account. This trade brought under my eyes a great number and variety of Cows from all quarters—from Switzerland, Holland, Brittany, Poitou, &c. &c.; and I had better opportunities than before for thoroughly examining the marks of these different races. My observations were multiplied, and I became convinced anew that all individuals possessing the same marks belonged to the same family, whatever might be the country of their birth; that these marks were an infallible indication of the same degree of superiority or inferiority; in a word, that Nature, always consistent with herself, acted, at all times and places, in the same way, and was always governed by the same laws.

For between seven and eight years, I had been incessantly engaged in establishing order among my observations, and arranging the results into one consistent whole. I established a classification, founded upon the shape or outline of the different marks: Cows were first divided into classes or families; then, in each of these classes, there was a threefold division, according to size—the *tall* or *high*, the *medium*, and the *low*; finally, each class was subdivided into orders, according to the diminution and the deformity of the distinctive mark of the class, as found in the different individuals belonging to it. This task was an immense one for me, and cost me a degree of trouble and an expenditure of time, of which a conception may be formed by considering how many comparisons and combinations were necessary to a person so unversed in scientific methods, before my materials could be reduced to order, and I could form a distinct and precise idea of my own discovery.

These difficulties, which might have disheartened any other person, did not discourage me. A system was to be created, and I created it. In 1828, I addressed to the Academy of Bordeaux a request, having for its object that my method should be examined and reported upon. I was not yet willing to disclose my secret entirely; my object was to get the reality of my discovery and its results attested to. The Academy, without adopting my conclusions, did nevertheless make honorable mention of me, at its sitting of the 3d of June following, in these terms:

"M. Francis Guénon, of Libourne, possessor of a method which he deems infallible for judging, by mere visual examination, of the goodness of Milch Cows, and the quantity of milk which each can yield, has solicited the Academy to cause the efficaciousness of this method to be tested by repeated experiments. The case presented by this request was one of a secret method of judging, which the possessor was not willing to reveal. On the other hand, it seemed difficult to admit that the external signs, whatever they might be, by which M. Guénon judges, could always bear a proportional relation to the quantity of milk yielded by a Cow. Nevertheless, the Academy deemed it proper to appoint a Committee charged with making the examination.

"Trials have been made, with the care and under the precautions necessary for precluding all collusion. The Cows used for the purpose belonged to three different herds, and amounted to thirty in number, and the result has been to establish, to the satisfaction of the Committee, that M. Guénon really possesses great sagacity in this line. So long, however, as his method shall be kept secret, it cannot be judged of nor rewarded by the Academy.

"Governed by these considerations, the Academy, having ascertained from M. Guénon that he is willing to submit to every test that may be proposed, and to disclose his secret upon receiving a just indemnity, has referred him to the Prefect, and has engaged to recommend him to the favorable notice of that magistrate, who is ever disposed to promote all that tends to improvement."

Here the matter rested at that time. I did not then make up my mind to give my secret to the public; but I persevered in my observations and experiments, in order to perfect my discovery. In 1837, the Agricultural Society of Bordeaux determined to ascertain for itself what reality there might be in my system.— The result surpassed its expectation; the experiments made, in presence of the Committee appointed for the purpose, left no doubt as to the certainty of my method. Here are the terms in which the Committee expressed themselves in their report:

AGRICULTURAL SOCIETY OF BORDEAUX.
GUENON DISCOVERY.... MILCH COWS.
Report to the Agricultural Society of Bordeaux.

Gentlemen: The Committee appointed by you to examine into the discoveries of M. Francis Guénon, of Libourne, have the honor to submit to you the result of their investigations.

M. Guénon has established a natural method, by means of which it is easy to recognize and class the different kinds of Milch Cows, according to

1st. *The quantity of milk which they can yield daily.*
2d. *The period during which they will continue to give milk.*
3d. *The quality of their milk.*

Down to the present day, Gentlemen, the writers and professors who have the most particularly occupied themselves with the bovine race have been unable to do anything more than indicate some vague signs for judging of the fitness of Cows for secreting milk.

After more than twenty years of observations and researches, M. Guénon has succeeded at length in discovering certain natural and positive signs, which constitute the basis of his method; a method henceforward proof against all error.

Sensible of the necessity that your Committee should be fully convinced, and that they could not but look with some degree of distrust upon any results of the proposed trials of his method, unless they should know that those results rested upon tangible facts, and were nowise dependent upon guess work, M. Guénon began by imparting his secret to your Committee, and making them fully acquainted with the positive signs upon which he has founded his method. By means of these signs, which are all external and apparent, he has established eight classes or families, which embrace all the varieties of the Cow that are to be met with in the different parts of this kingdom. Each of these classes or families is subdivided into eight orders. It is divided, also, into three sections, so that each of the sections comprehends the eight orders; this last division having reference merely to the size of the Cows, and serving to distinguish animals which, being the same in respect to the characteristic signs that serve to fix the class and the order to which they belong, differ in height alone, and in their yield so far only as this is dependent upon size.

By means of this classification, which is no less clear and distinct than simple, we are enabled,

1st. To distinguish with ease, in any herd of Cows, each individual comprised in it, according to the quantity of milk which she is capable of yielding—from twenty-six quarts a day down to next to nothing, and all intermediate quantities.

2d. To know the qualities of the milk which each will give, as being creamy or serous.

3d. To determine during what time, after being got with calf, the Cow will continue to give milk.

This method—so precious, from the application of which it is susceptible, whether we be concerned in the yield of milk only, or whether we avail ourselves of it for the improvement of breeds, which are constantly liable to deterioration from mismanagement in crossing—acquires a new interest when we consider that it is applicable, not to full grown animals alone, but also to calves at so early an age as three months. Thus, on the one hand, it affords the means of forming a sure judgment of full grown animals, in regard to which we are often misled, by their form and their parentage, to entertain great expectations which are never realized; and, on the other hand, it secures the improvement of herds, by enabling us to dispose at once of those calves which can never repay the trouble and cost of rearing them.

This important end, hitherto so vainly aimed at, had it at length been attained? To ascertain this point is the duty with which your Committee were charged. The method of M. Guénon having been revealed to them, it remained to ascertain how far the essential signs upon which it rests might be susceptible of rigorous application.

With this view they passed several days in visiting a number of pasture fields, situated in localities that differed from each other, in order that the experiments might be made upon animals of different breeds, and under varying circumstances. They deem it proper to enter here into some details respecting their mode of proceeding, persuaded that you will thereby be the better enabled to understand and appreciate the merits of this method, and to form a correct judgment of the extent to which your protection is due to a discovery, which is submitted to you by the author with the greater confidence, because it bears directly upon the prosperity of the agriculturist.

Every Cow subjected to examination was separated from the rest. What M. Guénon had to say in regard to her was taken down in writing by one of the Committee; and immediately after the proprietor, who had kept at a distance, was interrogated, and such questions put to him as would tend to confirm or disprove the judgment pronounced by M. Guénon. In this way we have examined, in the most careful manner—note being taken of every fact and every observation made by any one present—upward of sixty Cows and Heifers; and we are bound to declare that every statement made by M. Guénon with respect to each of them, whether it regarded the quantity of milk, or the time during which the Cow continued to give milk after being got with calf, or, finally, the quality of the milk as being more or less creamy or serous, was confirmed, and its accuracy fully established. The only discrepancies which occurred were some slight differences in regard to the *quantity* of milk; but these, as we afterward fully satisfied ourselves, were caused entirely by the food of the animal being more or less abundant.

The results of this first test seemed conclusive; but they acquired new force from those of a second trial, in which the method was subjected to another test, through M. Guénon and his brother. Your Committee, availing themselves of the presence of the latter, caused the same Cows to be examined by the two brothers, but separately; so that, after a Cow had been inspected, and her qualities, as indicated by the signs in question, had been pronounced upon by one of the brothers, he was made to withdraw; then the other brother, who had kept aloof, was called up, and desired to state the qualities of the same animal. This mode of proceeding could not fail to give rise to differences—to contradictions, even—between the judgments of the two brothers, unless their method was a positive and sure one. Well! Gentlemen, we must say it—this last test was absolutely decisive: not only did the various judgments of the two brothers accord perfectly together, but they were in perfect accordance, also, with all that was said by the proprietors in regard to the qualities, good and bad, of every animal subjected to this examination.

To the proprietors and to the bystanders, all this was the more surprising, from the fact that the examination was no less prompt than its results were certain. It was, however, easy to perceive that they, ignorant as they were of the nature of the discovery, had but little confidence in it; and that they ascribed the cunning of M. Guénon simply to a great practical familiarity with Cows.

As to ourselves—for whom, as we have already informed you, Gentlemen, the method was no longer a secret—it was with constantly renewing feelings of interest and astonishment that we followed up these examinations and contemplated the accuracy of their results. Two members particularly of the Committee, whom their special pursuits and their physiological knowledge of domestic animals entitle to great confidence, had, from the very first examination, been struck with the truth and strength of the system, the successful applications of which were multiplying under our eyes. This system, Gentlemen, we do not fear to say it, is infallible. The signs upon which it is founded, ever constant, invariable in the place which they occupy, are strongly impressed upon the animal by the hand of Nature. To appreciate them becomes an easy task; all that is requisite being, after having examined the animal and ascertained what marks she bears, to examine the drawings and fix upon the one in which those same marks appear. Then, by means of a brief but precise explanation which refers to that drawing, the qualities of the animal under examination become known, and the class and order to which she naturally belongs are indicated. It is by proceeding thus—by examining, first, the marks upon the animal, and then seeking among the drawings for the one in which those marks were reproduced—that the members of your Committee, after witnessing the first experiment, have been able themselves to apply the system, and to form judgments which were afterward corroborated in the same way that those of M. Guénon were.

In the hight of our admiration, Gentlemen, it was a subject of lively regret that the whole Society were not present; but we have the consolation of hoping that each of you will soon experience the pleasure which we have enjoyed, and have it in his power to apply this discovery to his own use and benefit. M. Guénon is not disposed to keep it secret; he proposes, so soon as a list of three thousand subscribers shall have been filled, to publish a work, in which his system, completely developed, shall be placed in the strongest light. The distinctive signs of each class and each order will be exactly described, and accurately represented by engraved or lithographic drawings; and the quantity of milk which each description of Cow is capable of yielding will be stated.

By means of this faithful guide, which is within the capacity of every understanding, errors will be dispelled, and the ability to form correct judgments of Cows will become common to all classes o husbandmen. Before long, none but Cows and Bulls of the first order will be used to breed from; this race of animals, which has become degenerate through bad crosses, will be elevated; and, as in other species of domestic animals, individuals of pure blood will be readily obtainable. Then, guided by sure and positive knowledge respecting the future qualities of young Cattle, we shall no longer rear, at great expense for three or four years, a Calf whose secretion of milk can never be otherwise than small in quantity and poor in quality; while, on the other hand, we shall no longer blindly consign to the butcher, young animals that would repay all the care that could be bestowed upon them.

These considerations will, we feel persuaded, Gentlemen, determine you to encourage M. Guénon to the publication and dissemination of a method which promises to be so useful to the agriculturist. How many poor families, in the neighborhood of large cities, where there is always a great consumption of milk, find in a small number of Cows the means of their subsistence! How extensive a branch of trade is supported by the production of butter and cheese in many of our Provinces—Brittany, Normandy, the Pyrenees, and others! Holland and Switzerland, those countries of fine pastures, are they not indebted to this branch of husbandry for a prosperity which is ever reproducing itself, and never wearing out—a prosperity less rapid, less brilliant, perhaps, than that which results from adventurous traffic, but safer at least for those who depend upon it; which is never deceptive; which, more than any other, attaches man to his country, and favors morality, and seems sheltered from those political tempests which, in other lands, so often prostrate the tallest fortunes.

[Signed] GUICHENET, *Veterinary Professor of the Department.*
LECONTE,
F. PELISSIER.

After the reading of this Report, the Society decreed as follows:
1st. That a gold medal be awarded to M. Francis Guénon.
2d. That he be proclaimed a Member of this Society.
3d. That fifty copies of his work on Milch Cows be subscribed for.
4th. That a thousand copies of the Report be printed for distribution among the Agricultural Societies of France.

The foregoing proceedings took place at the General Meeting of the Society, at the House of the Prefecture, on the 4th of July.

A true extract.

[Signed]   RICHIER, *Secretary General of the Society.*

AGRICULTURAL SOCIETY OF AURILLAC.

At its General Meeting of the 26th May, the following Report was presented and read on the subject of the experiments which I had been called upon to make:

Report.

Gentlemen: M. Francis Guénon, a husbandman of Libourne, has established a method, deemed by him infallible, by means of which, upon a mere inspection of any Milch Cow, she may be judged of, and we may know the quality of her milk, the quantity of it which she is capable of yielding, and also the time during which she can give milk.

A Committee appointed by the Agricultural Society of Bordeaux, and composed of several well informed agriculturists, and of a very distinguished Professor of the Veterinary art of the Department of Gironde, had already borne testimony, after putting it to numerous tests, to the efficaciousness of the system of M. Guénon; and the result of its observations had been published in a very remarkable Report, addressed to all the Agricultural Societies of France.

Your Society, considering that this discovery might be of high importance to our country, which derives its income chiefly from the produce of Milch Cows, entered into correspondence with its author, and gladly accepted his obliging offer to come to Auvergne and subject his method to the test of experiment.

Yesterday, the 25th of May, M. Guénon arrived at Aurillac, and immediately proceeded with the members of your Committee to the *Veyrac* farm, belonging to the President of the Society.— He examined with the utmost care the fine cow stable of that domain, which embraces one hundred Cows, of the best varieties that we possess. He then began his experiments upon a number of Cows which were presented to him, and which had designedly been selected from among the best, the moderately good, and the most indifferent of the establishment. Upon each of these separately, M. Guénon pronounced with precision, both in regard to her daily yield of milk, and to the time during which she continued to give milk after being got with calf. We must acknowledge, Gentlemen, that his decisions corresponded almost invariably with the statements obtained from the persons in whose charge the Cows are. The only variances we had to notice were some very slight ones in regard to the quantity of milk. On this point, we must call your attention to the fact that the Cows of that establishment are always fed high, upon clover or other artificial grasses which considerably augment the quantity of milk; and that this may have caused the mistake of M. Guénon, which consisted in his pronouncing the yield to be a little less than it really is. It is to be remarked that he was totally unacquainted with the usages of the country in regard to the feeding of Cattle.

In order thoroughly to convince your Committee of the reality of the discovery, M. Guénon made us acquainted with the different signs upon which his method rests. With reference to these signs, which are external and apparent, and stamped by the hand of Nature upon each animal, he has established eight classes or families, that comprehend all the varieties of the Cow found in the various Provinces of France. Each class is divided into eight orders; and each of these orders into three sections, according to size, as being high, of medium hight, and low.

According to the numerous observations of the author, all Cows belong to some one of these classes or families, and take their place under some one of the eight orders of the class. Each class possesses marks differing in shape and size from those of the other classes; and these marks are easy to distinguish, on merely looking at them. In each class, the Cows of the first orders are the best of the class, and the yield of milk is in proportion to the order; so that the two higher orders are the most productive, the third and fourth orders tolerably good, and the others falling off more and more, according to their grade.

M. Guénon applied his system, in our presence, to a number of Cows which were presented to him a second time; he made us remark their various signs, which differed in size and shape, and were larger or smaller according as the Cow was a good or a bad milker. He informed us that his system is equally applicable to young animals, and that their future qualities in regard to the production of milk can be judged of with equal certainty. In corroboration of this, he caused us to notice the same signs upon Calves three or four months old, and also upon Bulls destined for the next covering season. The cowherds stated that the Calves which had been assigned by him to the first orders were from Cows that gave a great deal of milk. Upon two splendid Bulls, of the fine breed of SALERS, which were of the same age, and exactly alike in hair and size, M. Guénon passed very different judgments: the one he pronounced good, and assigned to the first order of his *Flanders* class; the other he pronounced bad, and assigned to the fifth order of his *Horizontal* class.* He justified these judgments by very precise comparisons, and made us remark the difference that existed in the signs of the two animals.

This day, the 26th of May, M. Guénon has made new experiments at the Cattle Fair of the town of Aurillac, in presence of several members of the Central Agricultural Society and of the Sub-Societies, and of a great number of land-owners and agriculturists of Cantal and the neighboring Departments. The following is the manner in which your Committee have thought proper to proceed. Each Cow was examined separately by M. Guénon, who wrote his notes upon her, and delivered the paper, closed, to one of us. Immediately after, another member of the Committee questioned the owner of the Cow, or the person in charge of her, in regard to her daily yield of milk, its quality, and the time during which she continued to give milk after being got with calf. The answers were taken down in writing, and then compared with the notes written by M. Guenon. They were generally found to accord, and proved, to the satisfaction of your Committee and of every one present—all of whom attended with lively interest to these proceedings— that M. Guénon possesses great sagacity in judging of Cattle, and that his method rests upon a sure foundation.

An incident occurred to confirm us in this opinion. A farmer played the trick of bringing up for examination a Cow that had already been examined and pronounced upon. The notes written by M. Guénon on this occasion accorded exactly, in every respect, with those he had written on the former.

The method of M. Guénon has not the merit of being a brilliant theory. It rests upon facts and long experience. It is only after repeated trials, and twenty-five years of toilsome researches, that its author has accomplished the task of establishing it.

We are of opinion, Gentlemen, that M. Guénon ought to be encouraged by you in the publication of a system which appears to us destined to exercise a happy influence on the advancement of one of the most important branches of rural economy. What immense advantages may there not result, particularly in Auvergne, where the raising of Cattle and the manufacture of cheese constitute the chief branch of industry, from a method which should enable us to distinguish, in a sure way, between good and bad Cows? By applying this system to Calves and to Bulls, our stock would rapidly be raised to a high point of excellence, and we should soon have in our mountains none but Cows of the best kind.

In view of all these considerations, your Committee have the honor to propose—

1st. *That there be awarded to M. Guénon a gold medal, with the effigy of* OLIVIER de SERRES.
2d. *That he be proclaimed a Corresponding member of the Society.*
3d. *To subscribe for twenty-five copies of his work, for distribution among the Sub-Societies of the department.*
4th. *To cause this Report to be inserted in the* AGRICULTURAL PROPAGATOR, *and to transmit a copy to all the Prefects and Agricultural Societies of France.*

[Signed]   COUNT SAIGNES,
G. DE LALAUBIE,
GENERAL BARON HUGONET,
V. DE PRUINES, *Reporter of the Committee.*

Note.—At the same sitting, the recommendations of the Committee were adopted by the Central Society of Agriculture of Cantal.

With this highly flattering testimony in hand, I now come forward to publish the result of my silent meditations and toilsome studies. Every one will be able, with the aid of the lithographic drawings attached to the work, readily to recognize the distinctive marks of the animal examined by him. These marks are visible upon the posterior part of every Cow, in the space embraced between the

---

* See the names of the several classes, in the chapter *On the different kinds of Cows.*

udder and the vulva. They consist of a kind of escutcheons of various shapes and sizes, formed by the hair growing in different directions, and bounded by lines where these different growths of hair meet. The varieties of these escutcheons mark the different classes and orders of Cows.

It is upon these signs that every one may rest his judgment, by attending to the remarks contained in the body of the work upon the different kinds of Cows.— They are what every body has seen, or been able to see; but what no one has attended to. For myself, I have persevered through all obstacles: neither fruitless expenses, which were enormous for one of my means; nor the malice of the malevolent; nor the cold reception of the indifferent; nor the smile of incredulity; nothing has been able to damp my zeal. Strong in my conviction, I have been sustained by it through all my trials; and it has always raised me up when all conspired to depress me.

CHAPTER II.
ON THE DIFFERENT KINDS OF COWS.

§ 1. Genuine Cows.

I HAVE, as I said, established a classification of Cows; and the reader will have become aware how much time it must have cost me to arrive at this classification. Neither the language of Science nor its method is to be expected in my work: I have had no other instructor than myself, and Nature has been my only book. I am not pretending to write a treatise of Natural History; I am only giving to the public the result of my experience and observation. The suggestions of my own mind at the different stages of my discovery have been my only guides. In following up my observations, it was requisite that order should be established among the facts noticed by me and the thoughts to which they gave rise. To designate the various figures of the escutcheons of the several classes, new names were necessary. This order and this nomenclature are of my own invention.— For the purpose of coining French names, I have not ransacked Greek or Latin vocabularies; I have adopted those which suggested themselves as naturally expressive. If they be not formed after the rules of etymology, they are at least such as every one can seize the meaning of; and my book being destined chiefly for that class of men who are for the most part strangers to belles-lettres, it will possess in their eyes the merit of not disguising things under the words used to dignify them.

I divide Cows into *Eight* CLASSES or families; and these classes each into eight ORDERS. In each class, I distinguish three different SIZES; the *High*, the *Low* and the *Medium*. This classification embraces all kinds of Cows known to me; every individual being assignable to some one of these eight classes, and to some one of the orders comprised in it. According to the *Class*, the *Order*, and the *Size* of an animal, is her yield of milk: this being always found to correspond with the escutcheon characteristic of each class; some one of which escutcheons, is recognized in every Cow, more or less perfectly defined and free from blemish, according to the degree in which she approaches to the perfection of her class. This mark consists, as I have said, of the figure, on the posterior parts of the animal, formed by the meeting of the hair that grows or points in different directions; the line of junction of these different growths of hair constituting the outline of the figure or escutcheon. Here are the names of the eight classes:

1st Class....THE FLANDERS COW.	5th Class....THE DEMIJOHN COW.	
2d " .... " BELVAGE COW.	6th " .... " SQUARE SCUTCHEON COW.	
3d " .... " CURVELINE COW.	7th " .... " LIMOUSINE COW.	
4th " .... " BICORN COW.	8th " .... " HORIZONTAL CUT COW.	

By means of the following description of the several Classes and Orders, aided by the engraved prints attached to the work, every person can assign any Cow examined by him to her appropriate place in the classification, and consequently form an accurate judgment in regard to the maximum quantity of milk which she can yield daily, and also to the time during which this yield will remain at its maximum. It results from the numerous and oft-repeated tests to which this method of judging has been subjected, that the yield may sometimes vary from what I have adopted as the standard point; because, as I have stated, the climate, the food and the season do exercise an influence upon it. But there is one thing which never varies, which always holds good, at all times and in all places: in every one of the eight classes, the Cows of the higher orders are always the best, and those of the lower orders always the least good; that is to say, the two highest orders are always the most productive, the third and fourth orders are tolerably good, and the four others go on diminishing to the last, which may be looked upon as nullities so far as regards milk.

§ 2. Bastard Cows.

Before entering upon a detailed description of the classes severally, it is important that the reader be reminded that each class has its *Bastards*; that is to say, Cows which, although bearing a perfect resemblance to the others, do nevertheless differ from them in their yield. This resemblance deceives the most practiced eye, and is the source of many mistakes and of serious losses. In order, therefore, that the reader may be enabled to avail himself of my method, I must make him acquainted with the marks by which the bastards of each class are distinguished.

I have adopted the word *Bastard* to denote those Cows which give milk only so long as they have not been got with calf anew; and which, upon this happening, go dry, all of a sudden or in the course of a few days. Cows of this kind are found in each of the classes, and in every order of the class. Some of them are great milkers; but so soon as they have got with calf, their milk is gone. Others present the most promising appearance, but their yield is very insignificant. Cases of this kind occur every day; the most skillful judges find themselves mistaken.

When it happens that a Cow that was giving a plenty of milk loses it, all of a sudden, upon being got with calf, people do not know how to account for this loss of her milk; various causes are assigned for it, not one of which is the true one. It does not depend, as some suppose, upon the will of the animal about letting down her milk; it so happens simply because she is born so, because she is so formed and constituted.

Now there are characteristic signs, also, whereby the Bastard Cows in each of the classes and orders may be known. They are distinguished by the lines of ascending and descending hair in their escutcheon. These escutcheons are put before the reader's eyes in the Ninth plate, the drawings of which are, like the others, from nature.

In general, these Bastard Cows conceive with great facility the first time they come in heat, if they be then put to the bull. But they do not continue to give milk in any quantity; they cannot furnish enough even for the calf. Consequently if a Cow of this kind be put to the bull, it becomes necessary to wean her calf, and it falls away so as to be unfit for the butcher.

Among the Bastard Cows, some yield an oily and creamy milk; others but a serous milk: some give a great deal; others but little. In them, as in the genuine Cow of the same classes, the yield varies with the size; and the color of the dandruf is the same.

Generally speaking, the flow of milk is at its maximum during the first eight days after calving; but the milk is of a bad quality. After this period it undergoes a slight diminution; but its flow being once regularly established, the quantity remains constant until the Cow has conceived anew. At this period, it undergoes another diminution, in all the Classes and Orders; but more or less according to the Class and Order. We are now to enter into a more particular explanation of this.

CLASS I.

The Flanders Cow.

The reader is already apprised that, in the denominations which have suggested themselves to me, he is not to expect etymological or scientific combinations. The names which I have given to my classes are altogether arbitrary, and have reference to my own notions solely. I have adopted the above appellation for the Cows of my first class, which are the best in our country, because Cows of the Flemish breed, extensively known for their valuable qualities, possess, generally speaking, the escutcheon which is characteristic of this first class. These Cows, which I call the *Flanders* Cows, are the best milkers; they are also, among us, the most scarce. In this class, as in all the others, each order is distinguished by a particular modification of the general mark or escutcheon of the class; and there is a corresponding difference in the yield of milk, in the proportions which I am about to specify.

With respect to *size*, I call a Cow *high* when she weighs from five to six hundred pounds; of *medium hight*, when she weighs from three to four hundred pounds; *low*, when she weighs from one to two hundred pounds.*

HIGH COW.... First Order.

Cows of the First Order of this class and this size yield, whilst at the hight of their flow, (that is to say, from the time of calving until they are got with calf again) *twenty litres*† of milk a day. After they have conceived anew, the quantity of milk diminishes little by little; but they continue to give milk until they are eight months gone with calf: indeed Cows of this order never go dry, if we choose to milk them all the time.

Cows of this Class and Order are known by their having a delicate udder, covered with a fine, downy hair growing upward from between the four teats. This downy growth extends upward, over the hinder part of the udder and the region above it, blending itself with a similar growth (of hair pointing upward) which, beginning on the legs, a little above the hock joint, covers the inner sur-

* This is French weight. To reduce it to English avoirdupois, add 8 pounds to every 100.
† The *litre* is one of the modern French measures, containing about 2¼ English wine pints

54 TREATISE ON MILCH COWS.

Table I.....Class 1.
THE FLANDERS COW.

Order 1st.

Order 2d.

Order 5th.

Order 6th.

𝕮able I.....𝕮lass 1.

THE FLANDERS COW.

Order 3d.

Order 4th.

Order 7th.

Order 8th.

face of the thighs, encroaching upon the outer surface to the points A A, (Plate 1, Order I,) and then contracting as it extends upward to the points B B, on each side of the vulva, and about four inches* distant from it. They generally have, above the hind teats, two small oval marks, formed by hair growing downward, each of which is about two inches wide by three inches long. These marks are distinguishable also by their color, which is paler than that of the surrounding upward-growing hair.

In the First Order of this Class, the skin of the inner surface of the thighs and adjacent parts, up to the vulva, is of a yellowish color, with here and there a black spot. A sort of bran or dandruf detaches from it.

All Cows whose escutcheon corresponds, in its general shape or outline, with the one here described and seen in the plate, modified as it is in the various Orders, belong to this Class, whatever may be their color or their breed.

SECOND ORDER.—Cows of this Order yield, while at the hight of their flow, *eighteen litres* a day; and they continue to give milk until they are eight months gone with calf.

The marks of this Order are exactly like those of the First Order, (they are designated in the Plate by the same letters,) except that to the right of the vulva and near it there is a streak of hair growing downward (F). This mark is about four-tenths of an inch wide by two and a half inches long; the hair within it is very short. It indicates that the daily yield of the Cow diminishes by about one-sixth, upon her being got with calf.

THIRD ORDER.—Cows of this Order yield, while at the hight of their flow, *sixteen litres* a day, and continue to give milk until they are seven months gone with calf.

Their escutcheon resembles in shape that of the preceding Orders. It differs therefrom in having within it a semi-circle (C) of downward-growing hair, embracing the vulva and extending about one and a half inches below it, while it is about two and a half inches in width. The hair within this semi-circle is more shining and of a lighter color than the ascending hair around. In this Order there is but one oval (E) above the teats, to the left.

FOURTH ORDER.—Cows of this Order yield, while at the hight of their flow, *fourteen litres*, and continue to give milk until six months gone with calf.

The escutcheon differs from those above described in being more contracted—the upward-growing hair occupying less surface. The points A A are not so far apart, and consequently nearer to the inside of the thighs. The points B B are nearer to the vulva—distant from it only about four-tenths of an inch. From these points there is a growth of downward-growing hair, which encloses the vulva, forming with it the two triangles seen in the Plate, one side of which is B C. These triangles also are distinguishable by the hair being more lustrous and of a lighter color.

FIFTH ORDER.—Cows of this Order yield, while at the hight of their flow, *twelve litres* a day, and continue to give milk until they are five months gone with calf.

The escutcheon of this Order, as compared with that of the preceding, is somewhat narrower at the points A A and B B. Below the vulva, there is a streak of descending hair (C) about six inches long by a little over one inch wide. This

---

* The French measures, which are given in the fractions of the *metre*, have been reduced to English inches. The reduction is not, in every instance, absolutely exact; but it is sufficiently so for practical purposes.

escutcheon is distinguished also by a growth of descending hair (G) on the right thigh, which, beginning at A, encroaches upon the ascending hair, running into the inner surface of the thigh, to the distance of about six inches.

SIXTH ORDER.—Cows of this Order yield, during the hight of their flow, *nine litres* a day, and continue to give milk until four months gone with calf.

The escutcheon of this Order has the same figure as that of the Fifth, only it is more contracted at the points A A. On both thighs there is a growth of descending hair (G G), which runs into the inner surface of the thigh, forming a triangle, the sides of which are about four inches and two inches in length.—Below the vulva is the same mark (C) as in the preceding Order.

SEVENTH ORDER.—Cows of this Order yield, while at the hight of their flow, *six litres* a day, and continue to give milk until three months gone with calf.

In this Order, as is seen in the Drawing, the upper part of the escutcheon is entirely wanting on the right side. On the left side it is well defined, though on a very contracted scale, between the points A and B. On the right side, the lower portion of the escutcheon terminates at a point in the line where the two thighs join; that is to say, in a line with the vulva. To the right of this line, the only trace of the wanting half of the escutcheon, above the point just mentioned, consists in a few hairs bristling up against each other.

In this Order the udder is generally covered with a thin growth of coarse hair.

EIGHTH ORDER.—Cows of this Order yield, while at the hight of their flow, *four litres* a day, and continue to give milk until two months gone with calf.

The escutcheon is the same as that just described, only yet more contracted and imperfect. Here and there, on each side, a few scattering hairs bristle up within the space occupied by the escutcheon in the more perfect Orders.

What has been said of the distinctive marks of the several Orders of this Class holds good, whatever may be the size of the Cow, except that the *dimensions* above given, having reference to tall Cows, are to be proportionally reduced in regard to those of the other two sizes. Respecting the latter, therefore, it is requisite to state only their yield and the time during which they continue to give milk.

COW OF MEDIUM HIGHT.

FIRST ORDER.—Cows of the First Order of this Size yield, during the hight of their flow, *sixteen litres* a day; and, like those of the High Size, they continue to give milk until they are eight months gone with calf—the yield gradually diminishing from the time they conceive anew.

SECOND ORDER.—These Cows yield *fourteen litres* a day, and continue to give milk until seven months gone with calf.

THIRD ORDER.—These Cows yield *twelve litres* a day, and continue to give milk until six months gone with calf.

FOURTH ORDER.—These Cows yield *ten litres* a day, and continue to give milk until five months gone with calf.

FIFTH ORDER.—These Cows yield *eight litres* a day, and continue to give milk until four months gone with calf.

SIXTH ORDER.—These Cows yield *five litres* a day, and continue to give milk until three months gone with calf.

SEVENTH ORDER.—These Cows yield *three litres* a day, and continue to give milk until two months gone with calf.

EIGHTH ORDER.—These Cows yield *two litres* a day, and they continue to give milk only until they have conceived anew.

LOW COW.

FIRST ORDER.—Cows of the First Order of this Size yield, while at the hight of their flow, *twelve litres* a day; and they continue to give milk until they are eight months gone with calf—the yield gradually diminishing from the time they conceive anew.

SECOND ORDER.—These Cows yield *ten litres* a day, and continue to give milk until seven months gone with calf.

THIRD ORDER.—These Cows yield *eight litres* a day, and continue to give milk until six months gone with calf.

FOURTH ORDER.—These Cows yield *six litres* a day, and continue to give milk until five months gone with calf.

FIFTH ORDER.—These Cows yield *four litres* a day, and continue to give milk until four months gone with calf.

SIXTH ORDER.—These Cows yield *three litres* a day, and continue to give milk until two months gone with calf.

SEVENTH ORDER.—These Cows yield *two litres* a day, and continue to give milk until one month gone with calf.

EIGHTH ORDER.—These Cows yield *one litre* a day, and continue to give milk only until they have conceived anew.

BASTARD OF THE FLANDERS COW.

Upon entering on the description of these Bastards, I will observe that I shall confine myself to Cows of the High Size; because, to apply the description to those of the smaller sizes, all that will be requisite is to reduce the dimensions of the marks in proportion to the smallness of the Cow.

The Flanders Cow has two varieties of Bastards, (Plate IX, Fig. 1 and 2.)— The first has, within the escutcheon of ascending hair, an oval (J) of downward-growing hair, just below the vulva, and in a line with it, distant therefrom about eight inches. This oval is about four inches long, by about two and a half inches wide; and the hair within it is invariably of a lighter color than that around.— The larger the oval is, the more rapidly will the Cow lose her milk and go dry upon being got with calf. The smaller it is, the less rapid will be the loss of milk; but it will not the less certainly take place, in a notable degree, in every Cow that bears this mark. It will be perceived that the Drawing represents the Cow of the First Order only—this being sufficient to make the reader well enough acquainted with the mark to recognize it when it occurs in Cows of the inferior Orders.

The Bastard No. 2 may be known by the circumstance that the upward-growing hair which forms the escutcheon, instead of lying smooth and pointing straight upward, bristles up like the beards of an ear of wheat, and projects crosswise over the outline of the escutcheon at the points A A. The more extensive the surface of the escutcheon is, and the finer and smoother the hair growing within it, the more abundant is the yield of milk. When this hair is coarse, long and scanty, it indicates a thin, serous milk.

In the Bastards, the skin on the interior of the thighs, up to the vulva, is generally of a reddish color; it is smooth to the touch, and yields no dandruf.

CLASS II.

The Selvage Cow.

The shape of the escutcheon of this Class is very different from that of the First. The upper part of this escutcheon consists, as is seen in the Drawing, (Plate II.) of a growth of ascending hair, rising vertically, and without any interruption from descending hair, to the vulva. Its resemblance to the list or selvage of a piece of cloth is what suggested the name that I have given to this Class.

HIGH COW.

FIRST ORDER.—Cows of this Order yield, during the hight of their flow, *eighteen litres* a day, and continue to give milk until they are eight months gone with calf. Like those of the First Order of the First Class, they never go dry, if we choose to milk them all the time.

The udder is delicate and covered with a fine, downy hair, growing upward.— The escutcheon consists of a growth of ascending hair, commencing between the fore teats, and also on the inner surface of the thighs just above the hock joint. It expands as it extends upward, till it reaches the points A A. Here it is bounded by a right line, which runs across the inner side of the thigh, from A A to the points D D, which are about four inches distant from each other. From these points right lines rise vertically to the vulva, where they terminate, about an inch and a half apart.

Above the two hind teats, and nearly in a vertical line with them, are two oval marks (E E), formed by a growth of descending hair, distinguishable by its lustre, the size of which is about the same as in the Flanders Cow.

In these Cows, also, the skin of the inner surface of the thighs is of a yellowish color.

SECOND ORDER.—These Cows yield, while at the hight of their flow, *sixteen litres* a day, and continue to give milk until seven and a half months gone with calf.

The escutcheon is the same as that of the First Order, only the points A A are not so high up, and the entire figure is on a rather smaller scale. To the left of the vulva, outside of the escutcheon, is a small streak of ascending hair (E), about two and three-fourths inches long by less than half an inch wide. There is but one oval above the hind teats, on the left side. The entire escutcheon is distinguishable by the hair within being more glossy than that around it.

THIRD ORDER.—These Cows yield, while at the hight of their flow, *fourteen litres* a day, and they continue to give milk until they are six months gone with calf.

The escutcheon differs from the preceding in the following particulars: it is on a smaller scale; the points A A are nearer to the points D D, and the lines which rise from the latter points meet at the vulva, so as to form an acute angle. On each side of the vulva is a streak of ascending hair (F F,) of the same size as the one in the preceding order; that on the right being, however, sensibly shorter than the one on the left. There is, also, but one of the oval marks (E) above the teats, to the left.

FOURTH ORDER.—These Cows yield, while at the hight of their flow, *twelve litres* a day, and continue to give milk until they are four and a half months gone with calf.

Table II.....Class 2.
THE SELVAGE COW.

Order 1st.	Order 2d.

Order 5th. 	Order 6th.

Table II.....Class 2.
THE SELVAGE COW.

Order 3d.

Order 4th.

Order 7th.

Order 8th.

The escutcheon is like that of the preceding order, with the difference that the points A A are considerably lower down than the points D D. The two streaks of ascending hair, on the right and left of the vulva, are longer by nearly an inch, and also wider than in the Third Order; and there is no oval mark above the teats.

FIFTH ORDER.—These Cows yield, during the hight of their flow, *ten litres* a day, and continue to give milk until they are three months gone with calf.

The escutcheon is on a smaller scale than in the Fourth Order; the points D D are much nearer together—the distance between them being less than one inch; the list or selvage, as it rises toward the vulva, takes a turn to the left—its width contracting very much—and runs up, past the lower extremity of the vulva, to the point F. There is but one streak of ascending hair (F) on the right of the vulva, six inches long by an inch and a half wide.

SIXTH ORDER.—These Cows yield, while at the hight of their flow, *eight litres* a day, and continue to give milk until they are two months gone with calf.

The escutcheon is yet more contracted than the one last described; the selvage is very narrow, and terminates in a point, about four inches from its base. There are two streaks of ascending hair, to the right and left of the vulva, of about the same size as the one in the fifth order; that is to say, six inches long by one and a half in width.

SEVENTH ORDER.—These Cows yield, during the hight of their flow, *six litres* a day, and continue to give milk until they are one month gone with calf.

The escutcheon is still smaller than the last; the selvage being now nothing more than a small angular projection of upward growing hair, in the direction of the vulva. There are two streaks of ascending hair (F F) on the right and left of the vulva. The one on the left is nearly eight inches long by an inch and a half wide; and consists of coarse hair, which, in growing upward, deflects crosswise toward the outer part of the thigh. The one on the right is of the same width, but only half as long as the other; it consists of hair growing in the same way.

EIGHTH ORDER.—These Cows yield, during the hight of their flow, *four litres* a day, and cease to give milk upon being got with calf.

The escutcheon is exceedingly small; the selvage is but a mere projecting point; there is but one streak at the side of the vulva, on the left; which is formed of a scanty growth of coarse hairs, bristling up and deflecting crosswise.

The remark made above, in regard to the First Class, I will here repeat with respect to the present and to the remaining six: all that is said of the different orders of the high size, so far as regards their characteristic marks, holds good of the same Orders in the other sizes, except as to the dimensions of the marks, which are to be proportionally reduced. On the subject of the two lower sizes, I shall therefore confine myself to the yield of milk, and the time during which the Cow continues to give milk after conceiving anew.

COW OF MEDIUM HIGHT.

FIRST ORDER.—These Cows yield, during the hight of their flow, *fourteen litres* a day, and continue to give milk until eight months gone with calf.

SECOND ORDER.—These Cows yield *thirteen litres* a day, and continue to give milk until six and a half months gone with calf.

THIRD ORDER.—These Cows yield *eleven litres* a day, and continue to give milk until five months gone with calf.

FOURTH ORDER.—These Cows yield *ten litres* a day, and continue to give milk until four months gone with calf.

FIFTH ORDER.—These Cows yield *eight litres* a day, and continue to give milk until three months gone with calf.

SIXTH ORDER.—These Cows yield *six litres* a day, and continue to give milk until two months gone with calf.

SEVENTH ORDER.—These Cows yield *four litres* a day, and continue to give milk until they have conceived anew.

EIGHTH ORDER.—These Cows yield *three litres* a day, and go dry upon being impregnated anew.

LOW COW.

FIRST ORDER.—These Cows yield, during the hight of their flow, *ten litres* a day; and continue to give milk until they are eight months gone with calf.

SECOND ORDER.—These Cows yield *eight litres* a day, and continue to give milk until they are six and a half months gone with calf.

THIRD ORDER.—These Cows yield *six litres* a day, and continue to give milk until five months gone with calf.

FOURTH ORDER.—These Cows yield *four litres* a day, and continue to give milk until four months gone with calf.

FIFTH ORDER.—These Cows yield *three litres* a day, and continue to give milk until three months gone with calf.

SIXTH ORDER.—These Cows yield *two litres* a day, and continue to give milk until two months gone with calf.

SEVENTH ORDER.—These Cows also yield *two litres* a day, but they go dry upon conceiving anew.

EIGHTH ORDER.—These Cows yield but *one litre* a day, and cease to give milk upon conceiving anew.

BASTARD OF THE SELVAGE COW

The Bastards of this Class, (see Plate IX. Fig. 3) whatever may be their size and the Order to which they belong, are to be known by two patches of ascending hair, (F F) on the right and left of the vulva, distant from it an inch and a quarter to an inch and a half. They are from four to five inches long by about an inch and a half wide. The smaller they are, and the finer the hair within them, the less rapid is the loss of milk which they always indicate. When they consist of coarse hair, and terminate in a point at each end, they indicate that the milk is poor and serous.

CLASS III.

The Curveline Cow.

I have given this name to the Cows of my Third Class, because their escutcheon, which is lozenge-shaped, is bounded above by two curved lines; which, commencing to the right and left on the thighs, run up toward the vulva, and meet at a point below it. (See Plate III.)

This Class is a very numerous one; and, in regard to the yield of milk, approximates to the First Class. Cows belonging to it, and to every one of its Orders,

64 TREATISE ON MILCH COWS.

Table III.....Class 3.
THE CURVELINE COW.

Order 1st. Order 2d.

Order 5th. Order 6th.

TREATISE ON MILCH COWS. 65

Table III.....Class 3.
THE CURVELINE COW.

Order 3d. Order 4th.

Order 7th.  Order 8th.

are found in all breeds. The yield varies according to the Order and the size, just as in the First and Second Classes.

HIGH COW.

FIRST ORDER.—Cows of this Size and Order yield, during the hight of their flow, *eighteen litres* a day, and continue to give milk until they are eight months gone with calf.

They exhibit the same delicacy of texture, and the same yellowish color of the skin within the escutcheon, as those of the higher Orders of the foregoing Classes. The escutcheon, in its upper part, is broader than that of the Second Class. It commences between the four teats, and on the inner surface of the thighs above the hock joint. Rising thence, and encroaching upon the outer surface of the thighs to two points, (A A) about midway up, its upper part is bounded by the lines above mentioned; which, beginning at the points A A, curve outward, and are united, just below the vulva, about an inch or less from it, by another short curved line. (B) The lower part of the escutcheon is bounded by lines on the thighs, curving inward.

Above the hind teats, and nearly in a vertical line with them, are two ovals, (E E) formed by hair growing downward, the same as in the higher Orders of the two preceding Classes.

SECOND ORDER.—These Cows yield, during the hight of their flow, *sixteen litres* a day, and continue to give milk until they are seven months gone with calf.

The escutcheon is the same as that just described, only somewhat contracted in all its parts. There is but one oval (E) above the teats, on the left side. On the left of the vulva, is a streak of ascending hair, (F) about an inch and a half long by less than half an inch in width.

THIRD ORDER.—These Cows yield, while at the hight of their flow, *fourteen litres* a day, and continue to give milk until six months gone with calf.

The escutcheon is of the same shape as in the preceding Order; contracted, however, in all its parts. The point B is still lower down. To the right and left of the vulva are two streaks of ascending hair, (F F) about four inches long by less than an inch in width. Above the teats, on the left, is one oval (E).

FOURTH ORDER.—These Cows, while at the hight of their flow, yield *twelve litres* a day, and continue to give milk until they are four months gone with calf.

The escutcheon is still the same in shape, but on a yet smaller scale throughout; its upper extremity at a greater distance, therefore, below the vulva. The base of its upper part rests on the udder. The streaks of ascending hair, (F F) on the right and left of the vulva, are longer and wider than those in the third Order; and the hairs within them bristle up, projecting on each side. On the right there is a failure of the ascending hair below the point A, and its place (F) is occupied by hair growing downward.

FIFTH ORDER.—These Cows, while at the hight of their flow, yield *ten litres* a day, and continue to give milk until they are three months gone with calf.

The escutcheon is smaller still, lower down, and confined to the inner surface of the thighs. On the left, there is a patch of bristling hair growing upward, nearly eight inches long by an inch and a half, or more, in width. To the right and left, beginning at the points A A, are two spaces (F F) covered with hair growing downward instead of the ascending hair. They are about four inches in width, and six inches long, running inward toward the crease formed by the meeting of the thighs.

SIXTH ORDER.—These Cows, while at the hight of their flow, yield *seven litres* a day, and continue to give milk until they are two months gone with calf.

The escutcheon is still of the same shape; but the point B is now so far down below the vulva that it must be looked for where the thighs meet. At the point E, under the vulva, is a small patch of ascending hair, about an inch and two-thirds long, by four-fifths of an inch in width.

SEVENTH ORDER.—These Cows, during the hight of their flow, yield *five litres* a day, and continue to give milk until they are impregnated anew.

The escutcheon is yet more reduced in size, and is now hid away between the thighs. To the right and left of the vulva, are two patches of ascending hair, (F F) which bristles up and projects on each side. They are about six inches long by two and a half wide.

EIGHTH ORDER.—These Cows yield, while at the hight of their flow, *three litres* a day, and go dry upon being got with calf.

In this Order, the escutcheon is still perceptible, but it is of a very diminutive size.

COW OF MEDIUM HIGHT.

FIRST ORDER.—These Cows yield, while at the hight of their flow, *fifteen litres* a day, and continue to give milk until they are eight months gone with calf.

SECOND ORDER.—These Cows yield *thirteen litres* a day, and continue to give milk until they are seven months gone with calf.

THIRD ORDER.—These Cows yield *eleven litres* a day, and continue to give milk until six months gone with calf.

FOURTH ORDER.—These Cows yield *nine litres* a day, and continue to give milk until five months gone with calf.

FIFTH ORDER.—These Cows yield *seven litres* a day, and continue to give milk until four months gone with calf.

SIXTH ORDER.—These Cows yield *five and a half litres* a day, and continue to give milk until three months gone with calf.

SEVENTH ORDER.—These Cows yield *three and a half litres* a day, and continue to give milk until two months gone with calf.

EIGHTH ORDER.—These Cows yield *two litres* a day, and go dry upon being got with calf.

LOW COW.

FIRST ORDER.—Cows of this Order and Size yield, while at the hight of their flow, *twelve litres* a day, and continue to give milk until they are eight months gone with calf.

SECOND ORDER.—These Cows yield *ten litres* a day, and continue to give milk until seven months gone with calf.

THIRD ORDER.—These Cows yield *eight litres* a day, and continue to give milk until six months gone with calf.

FOURTH ORDER.—These Cows yield *six litres* a day, and continue to give milk until five months gone with calf.

FIFTH ORDER.—These Cows yield *five litres* a day, and continue to give milk until four months gone with calf.

SIXTH ORDER.—These Cows yield *four litres* a day, and continue to give milk until three months gone with calf.

SEVENTH ORDER.—These Cows yield *three litres* a day, and go dry upon being impregnated anew.

Eighth Order.—These Cows yield *two litres* a day, and go dry upon being impregnated anew.

BASTARD OF THE CURVELINE COW.

In the Curveline Cow, the growths of ascending hair, (F F) to the right and left of the vulva, require special attention, in regard to their dimensions, to see that they are of the size indicated in the several descriptions of the different Orders. When they are of small size, they do not indicate a very rapid loss of milk; but when they are from four to five inches long, by an inch and a half in width, (in which case they are generally pointed at both ends, and consist of coarse hair,) they may then be considered as the size of a *bastard* Cow, that will go dry so soon as she is got with calf. As a general rule with regard to these marks, the larger they are, the worse will the Cow be in this respect. (See Plate IX. Fig. 4.)

CLASS IV.
The Bicorn Cow.

This name is given to my Fourth Class, because the upper part of its escutcheon represents two horns. Cows of this class are good milkers. They are found in all the breeds which we possess in France. In this, as in the other Classes, the general mark of the Class presents itself under modifications indicative of the Order to which the Cow belongs.

HIGH COW.

First Order.—Cows of this Order and Size yield, while at the hight of their flow, *sixteen litres* a day, and continue to give milk until they are eight months gone with calf.

Like those of the same Order in the foregoing Classes, they are distinguished by the delicacy of their udder. The dandruf which detaches from the skin throughout the escutcheon is of a yellowish or copperish color. This escutcheon, as I have said above, has at top two horns, formed in the way that is seen in the drawing. (Plate IV. Order 1.) It begins, as in the foregoing Orders, in the space between the four teats, and on the inner surface of the thighs, just above the hock joint; whence it rises toward the tail, spreading over the inner surface, and partially over the outer surface, of the thighs, to the points A A. From these points, its outline consists of curved lines to the points B B, which are distant about four inches from the vulva. Thence the outline descends again on each side in nearly straight lines, which meet at the point C, immediately beneath the vulva, and at the distance of about eight inches from it.* On the right and left of the vulva, are two streaks of ascending hair, (F F) about two inches long by two-fifths of an inch in width.

As in the higher Orders of the Classes already described, so in the present we find, above the two hind teats, two small oval marks, (D D) formed by hair growing downward in the field of ascending hair.

Second Order.—These Cows, while at the hight of their flow, yield *fourteen litres* a day, and continue to give milk until they are seven months gone with calf.

The escutcheon is the same as in the First Order; except that it is on a smaller scale, and does not reach so high up. The color of the skin within it is the same. Of the two streaks of ascending hair, (F F) on the right and left of the vulva, the one on the left is of the same size as in the First Order, whilst the other is but half as long. Of the two horns, (B B) the one on the right is upward of an inch shorter than the other. There is but one oval mark (D) above the teats, on the left.

THIRD ORDER.—These Cows, while at the hight of their flow, yield *twelve litres* a day, and continue to give milk until six months gone with calf.

The escutcheon is of the same shape as in the preceding Order; smaller, and consequently spreading less upon the outer surface of the thighs; the right hand horn shorter, by about two inches, than the one on the left. There is but one of the marks (F) along side of the vulva, on the left.

FOURTH ORDER.—These Cows, while at the hight of their flow, yield *ten litres* a day, and continue to give milk until five months gone with calf.

The escutcheon is smaller than in the Third Order; but the same in shape, except on the right of its lower part, when the following irregularity occurs: below the point A, the ascending hair is encroached upon by a growth of descending hair, that runs into the escutcheon, forming an angle, the point of which is at I I. Measured across from the point A, this angle of descending hair penetrates the escutcheon to the distance of about four inches; whilst the break which it makes in the outline of the escutcheon is from six to seven and a half inches long.

Besides this irregularity in the shape of the escutcheon, this Order is distinguished by a streak of ascending hair (E) under the vulva, nearly three inches long by two-fifths of an inch in width.

Whenever the blemish or irregularity in the escutcheon here described is found, it indicates a more rapid decrease in the daily yield of milk than would be exhibited by a Cow possessing the same escutcheon free from blemish; and the rate of decrease will be proportionate to the size of the blemish; that is to say, to the extent of surface covered by the descending hair where it encroaches upon the field of upward growing hair.

FIFTH ORDER.—These Cows, while at the hight of their flow, yield *eight litres* a day, and continue to give milk until they are four months gone with calf.

The escutcheon the same in shape as the preceding, but on a smaller scale. Near the vulva, to the left, is a streak of bristling hair, growing upward, (F) about six inches long by two wide. At the points A A, on the right and left, are two spaces where the ascending hair fails and is replaced by downward growing hair; which spaces penetrate the inner surface of the thighs to the points I I.

SIXTH ORDER.—These Cows yield, during the hight of their flow, *six litres* a day, and continue to give milk until three months gone with calf.

The escutcheon the same as in the Fifth Order; but smaller, and hid away between the thighs. Above it, to the right and left of the vulva, are two streaks (F F) of ascending hair, bristling up and projecting sideways. They are of the same size as the one in the preceding Order, just described.

SEVENTH ORDER.—These Cows yield, whilst at the hight of their flow, *four litres* a day, and continue to give milk until they are two months gone with calf.

The same escutcheon, but still more hid away between the thighs. The marks on the right and left of the vulva, consisting each of a growth of bristling

70 TREATISE ON MILCH COWS.

Table IV.....Class 4.
THE BICORN COW.

Order 1st.   Order 2d.

Order 5th.   Order 6th.

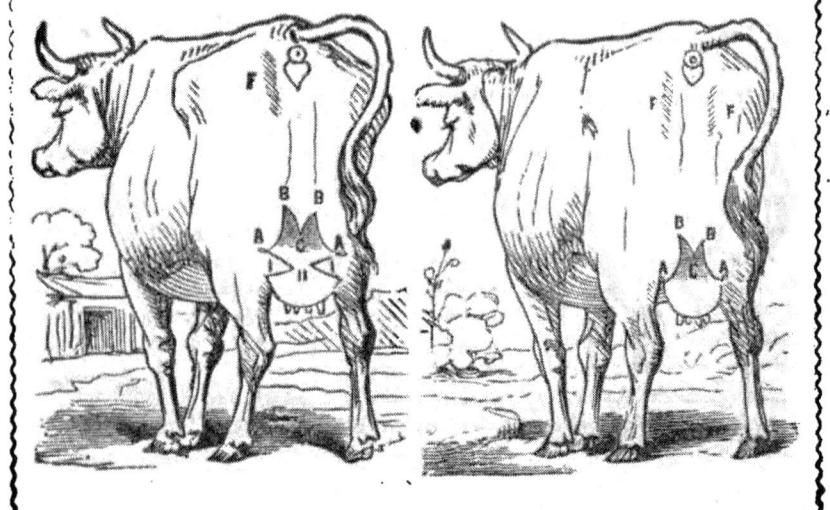

Table IV.....Class 4.
THE BICORN COW.

Order 3d. **Order 4th.**

Order 7th. **Order 8th.**

hair pointing upward, are longer and wider than those in the preceding Order the one on the right not so long as the other.

EIGHTH ORDER.—These Cows, while at the hight of their flow, yield *three litres* a day, and continue to give milk until they have conceived anew.

The escutcheon is still defined, but on a very small scale. If the marks of upward growing hair (F F) at the sides of the vulva exist at all, they consist of a few bristling hairs, projecting crosswise.

COW OF MEDIUM HIGHT.

FIRST ORDER.—Cows of this Order, while at the hight of their flow, yield *fourteen litres* a day, and continue to give milk until they are eight months gone with calf.

SECOND ORDER.—These Cows yield *twelve litres* a day, and continue to give milk until they are seven months gone with calf.

THIRD ORDER.—These Cows yield *ten litres* a day, and continue to give milk until six months gone with calf.

FOURTH ORDER.—These Cows yield *eight litres* a day, and continue to give milk until five months gone with calf.

FIFTH ORDER.—These Cows yield *six litres* a day, and continue to give milk milk until they are four months gone with calf.

SIXTH ORDER.—These Cows yield *four litres* a day, and continue to give milk until three months gone with calf.

SEVENTH ORDER.—These Cows yield *three litres* a day, and cease to give milk upon being got with calf.

EIGHTH ORDER.—These Cows yield still less, and go dry upon conceiving anew.

LOW COW.

FIRST ORDER.—These Cows yield, while at the hight of their flow, *eleven litres* a day; and continue to give milk until they are eight months gone with calf.

SECOND ORDER.—These Cows yield *nine litres* a day, and continue to give milk until seven months gone with calf.

THIRD ORDER.—These Cows yield *seven litres* a day, and continue to give milk until six months gone with calf.

FOURTH ORDER.—These Cows yield *five litres* a day, and continue to give milk until five months gone with calf.

FIFTH ORDER.—These Cows yield *four litres* a day, and continue to give milk until four months gone with calf.

SIXTH ORDER.—These Cows yield *three litres* a day, and continue to give milk until two and a half months gone with calf.

SEVENTH ORDER.—These Cows yield *two litres* a day, and their yield goes on diminishing until they conceive anew; at which time they go dry.

EIGHTH ORDER.—These Cows yield still less, and go dry at the same period.

BASTARD OF THE BICORN COW.

The marks F F possess the same properties for indicating the Bastards of this Fourth Class, as in regard to those of the Third. (See Plate IX. Fig. 5.)

CLASS V.

The Demijohn Cow.

This name indicates the shape of the escutcheon of this class. It may strike the reader as queer; but it is significant, and serves to recall the figure of the characteristic mark of the Class, which very much resembles the outline of a dem ijohn. If my discovery is a useful one, habit will soon accustom people to this name, as well as to the others of my Eight Classes; and to those who may feel disposed to find fault with them, 1 will say, what matters it to you? the name is as nothing, the importance is altogether in the thing.

HIGH COW.

FIRST ORDER.—Cows of this Order and Size, while at the hight of their flow, yield *sixteen litres* a day, and continue to give milk until they are eight months gone with calf.

The skin within the escutcheon has the same yellowish color as in the higher Orders of the preceding Classes. The udder is delicate, and covered with fine, downy hair. The escutcheon, consisting of a growth of ascending hair, begins between the four teats, and on the inner side of the legs, above the hock joint; as it extends upward it spreads upon the outer surface of the thighs to the points A A. (Plate V. Fig. 1.) From these points, the figure is bounded by right lines, to the points J J, which are distant from each other from five to six inches. From these points, the upward growing hair rises to the line N, where it is from two and a half to three and a quarter inches in width. This line is directly below the vulva, and distant from it about four inches. The wider the figure is at this place, and the nearer it approaches to the vulva, the better the Cow.

Above the hind teats are two ovals (E E), formed by descending hair, about four inches long, by nearly three inches in width. On the right and left of the vulva are two streaks of ascending hair (O O), nearly two and a half inches long, by less than half an inch in width. The hair within these streaks is fine and short, and very distinct from the descending hair that surrounds them.

SECOND ORDER.—These Cows yield, while at the hight of their flow, *fourteen litres* a day, and continue to give milk until they are seven months gone with calf.

The escutcheon differs from that of the First Order in being on a smaller scale. Above the teats there is but one oval (E), to the right, formed by descending hair. Of the two streaks of ascending hair (O O) alongside of the vulva, the one to the left is of the same dimensions as in the First Order; but the one to the right, although of the same width, is of but half the length.

THIRD ORDER.—These Cows, while at the hight of their flow, yield *twelve litres* a day, and continue to give milk until they are six months gone with calf.

The escutcheon, preserving its general shape, is yet more contracted. At the points A A, it is more rounded off, and no longer spreads on the outer surface of the thighs. Above the points J J, it is narrower; and it stops short at N considerably lower down beneath the vulva. There is but one of the streaks (O) of ascending hair, which is to the left of the vulva, and about an inch and a half long, by two-fifths of an inch in width.

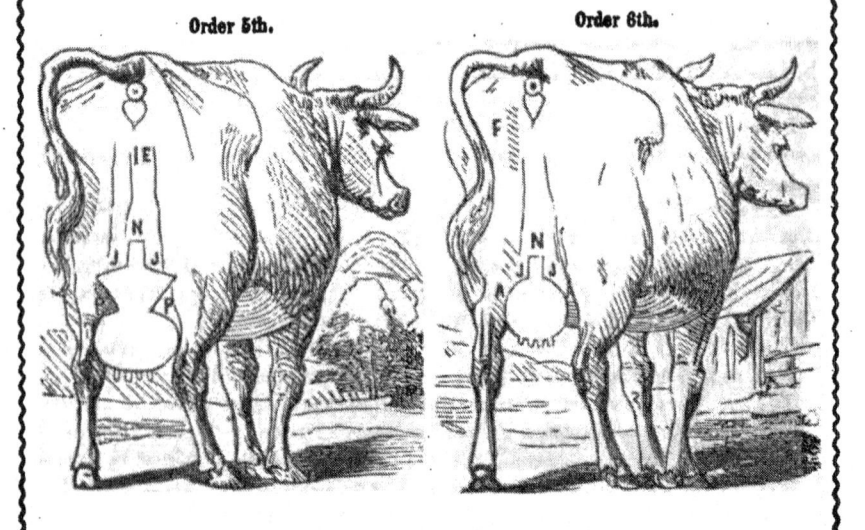

TABLE V.........CLASS 5.

The Demijohn Cow.

Order 1st.

Order 2d.

Order 5th.

Order 6th.

TREATISE ON MILCH COWS. 75

TABLE V.........CLASS 5.

The Demijohn Cow.

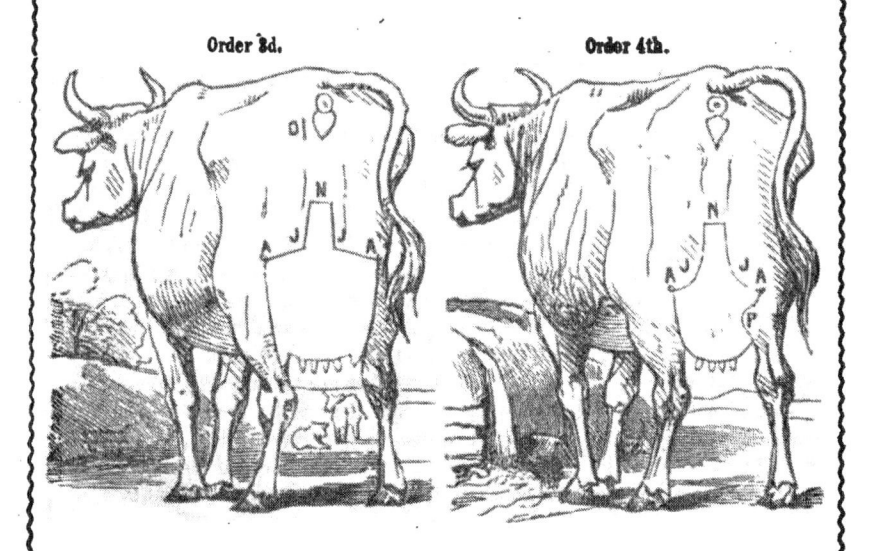

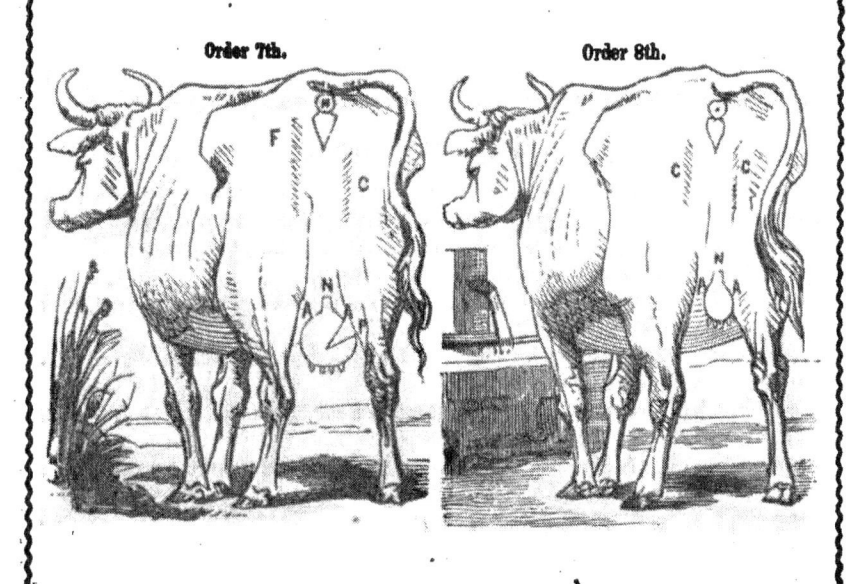

Order 3d.

Order 4th.

Order 7th.

Order 8th.

76 TREATISE ON MILCH COWS.

FOURTH ORDER.—These Cows, while at the hight of their flow, yield *ten litres* a day, and continue to give milk until they are five months gone with calf.

The escutcheon is yet more reduced in size. The points A A lower down and nearer together. The lines are more curved at the points J J, and the distance from these points to N is much less. Below A, on the right side, there is a failure of the upward growing hair, marked P.

FIFTH ORDER.—These Cows, while at the hight of their flow, yield *eight litres* a day, and continue to give milk until they are four months gone with calf.

The escutcheon goes on contracting in size. The points A A, being now on the inner surface of the thighs, are no longer so apparent. The upper extremity N is much farther below the vulva. At both points A A there is a failure of the ascending hair (P P), where its place is occupied by descending hair, running into the escutcheon. These marks are about five inches deep, by four in width.

Below the vulva there is a small streak of ascending hair (E), about an inch and a quarter long, by less than half an inch wide.

SIXTH ORDER.—These Cows, while at the hight of their flow, yield *six litres* a day, and continue to give milk until they are three months gone with calf.

The escutcheon is on a still more contracted scale than in the preceding Order. Near the vulva, to the left, there is a streak of ascending hair (F), which bristles up. It is nearly five inches long, by about one and a half in width.

SEVENTH ORDER.—These Cows, while at the hight of their flow, yield *four litres* a day, and continue to give milk until they are two months gone with calf.

The escutcheon is smaller and lower down than in the preceding Order. On the right and left of the vulva are two streaks of ascending hair, which bristles up. The one on the left (F) is somewhat longer than that found in the Sixth Order; the one on the right (C) is about four inches long, by an inch and a half in width. Below the point A, on the right hand, there is a failure of the ascending hair (P).

EIGHTH ORDER.—These Cows, while at the hight of their flow, yield *two litres* a day, and continue to give milk until they have conceived anew.

The escutcheon is hid away between the thighs; the points A A scarcely perceptible. The streaks of bristling hair (C C) on the right and left of the vulva are of the kind indicative of the degeneracy and bad quality of the Cow.

COW OF MEDIUM HIGHT.

FIRST ORDER.—These Cows, while at the hight of their flow, yield *fourteen litres* a day, and continue to give milk until they are eight months gone with calf.

SECOND ORDER.—These Cows yield *twelve litres* a day, and continue to give milk until they are seven months gone with calf.

THIRD ORDER.—These Cows yield *ten litres* a day, and continue to give milk until six months gone with calf.

FOURTH ORDER.—These Cows yield *eight litres* a day, and continue to give milk until five months gone with calf.

FIFTH ORDER.—These Cows yield *six litres* a day, and continue to give milk until four months gone with calf.

SIXTH ORDER.—These Cows yield *five litres* a day, and continue to give milk until three months gone with calf.

SEVENTH ORDER.—These Cows yield *three litres* a day, and continue to give milk until two months gone with calf.

EIGHTH ORDER.—These Cows yield still less, and go dry upon being got with calf.

LOW COW.

FIRST ORDER.—These Cows, while at the hight of their flow, yield *ten litres* a day, and continue to give milk until they are eight months gone with calf.

SECOND ORDER.—These Cows yield *eight litres* a day, and continue to give milk until seven months gone with calf.

THIRD ORDER.—These Cows yield *six and a half litres* a day, and continue to give milk until six months gone with calf.

FOURTH ORDER.—These Cows yield *five litres* a day, and continue to give milk until five months gone with calf.

FIFTH ORDER.—These Cows yield *four litres* a day, and continue to give milk until four months gone with calf.

SIXTH ORDER.—These Cows yield *three litres* a day, and continue to give milk until three months gone with calf.

SEVENTH ORDER.—These Cows yield *two litres* a day, and continue to give milk until two months gone with calf.

EIGHTH ORDER.—These Cows yield *one litre* of milk a day, and go dry upon conceiving anew.

BASTARD OF THE DEMIJOHN COW.

When the streaks marked F F are found in the Cow of this Class, of the dimensions specified in the description of the Bastard of the *Curveline* Cow, they serve here also to detect the Bastard Cow; and her badness in regard to the rapid loss of her milk will be in proportion to the size of these streaks. The smaller they are, the less defective will she be in this respect. (See Plate IX. Fig. 6.)

CLASS VI.

The Square-Scutcheon Cow.

The name indicates the appearance of the escutcheon, the upper part of which is shaped like a carpenter's or mason's square.

HIGH COW.

FIRST ORDER.—Cows of this Order and Size yield, while at the hight of their flow, *sixteen litres* a day, and they continue to give milk until they are eight months gone with calf.

The skin within the escutcheon is of the same yellowish color as in the superior Orders of the preceding Classes. The udder delicate, covered with short, fine hair. The escutcheon begins as in the foregoing Classes; and, rising from just above the hock joint, on the inner surface of the thighs, spreads outward to the points A A. (See Plate VI. Order 1.) Above those points it represents a square. A right line runs across to the points J J, distant from each other from five to six inches. Thence the figure is bounded by two right lines, which meet in an acute angle at the point E, distant about two inches from the vulva. Above that, to the left, the figure of a square is formed by two streaks of hair, E B and B C (the point C being at the orifice of the vagina); the former of which is about four inches long, by an inch and a quarter wide, and the latter from five to six inches long, by somewhat less than the same width.

Above the hindmost teats are two small oval marks (G G), formed by downward growing hair in the field of ascending hair. They are about five or six inches long, by two and a half wide. The hair within them is of a lighter color than that without.

The nearer the escutcheon approaches to the vulva, the better the Cow.

SECOND ORDER.—These Cows yield, while at the hight of their flow, *fourteen litres* a day, and continue to give milk until they are seven months gone with calf.

The escutcheon is the same as in the First Order, only somewhat reduced in size. The square figure near the vulva commences lower down, and is longer than the one just described. There is but one oval above the teats, to the left (G), of the same size as those in the First Order.

THIRD ORDER.—These Cows, while at the hight of their flow, yield *twelve litres* a day, and continue to give milk until they are six months gone with calf.

The escutcheon is the same in its general shape, but it is more contracted in all its parts, and does not extend so high up. The points A A are nearer to the inner surface of the thighs; and the escutcheon is narrower at the points J J, where the outline has acquired a curved character.

The angular space between J J and E is narrower than the streak E B, and shorter than B C. The latter is wider and longer than in the preceding Order.

FOURTH ORDER.—These Cows yield, while at the hight of their flow, *ten litres* a day, and continue to give milk until they are five months gone with calf.

The escutcheon is still more reduced in size. To the right of the vulva there is a streak of bristling hair, growing upward (F), about four inches long, by one and a half wide. Below the point A, to the right, there is a space (U) where the upward growing hair fails, and is replaced by descending hair.

FIFTH ORDER.—These Cows, while at the hight of their flow, yield *eight litres* a day, and continue to give milk until they are four months gone with calf.

The unfavorable marks are the same as in the preceding Order, only more conspicuous and on a larger scale.

SIXTH ORDER.—These Cows, while at the hight of their flow, yield *six litres* a day, and continue to give milk until they are three months gone with calf.

The escutcheon is yet more contracted, confined to the inner surface of the thighs, and more distant from the vulva. To the right and left of this orifice are streaks or lines of ascending hair, coarse and bristling.

SEVENTH ORDER.—These Cows, while at the hight of their flow, yield *four litres* a day, and continue to give milk until they are two months gone with calf.

The escutcheon is smaller still. The streak of ascending hair (F) on the right is wider, and the hair more bristling.

EIGHTH ORDER.—These Cows yield, while at the hight of their flow, *two litres* a day, and go dry upon being got with calf.

The shape of the escutcheon is still perceptible; but it is very small, and hid away between the thighs.

COW OF MEDIUM HIGHT.

FIRST ORDER.—These Cows, while at the hight of their flow, yield from *twelve* to *thirteen litres* a day, and they continue to give milk until they are eight months gone with calf.

SECOND ORDER.—These Cows yield *ten litres* a day, and continue to give milk until seven months gone with calf.

TREATISE ON MILCH COWS. 79

THIRD ORDER.—These Cows yield *eight litres* a day, and continue to give milk until six months gone with calf.

FOURTH ORDER.—These Cows yield *six litres* a day, and continue to give milk until five months gone with calf.

FIFTH ORDER.—These Cows yield *four and a half litres* a day, and continue to give milk until four months gone with calf.

SIXTH ORDER.—These Cows yield *three and a half litres* a day, and continue to give milk until three months gone with calf.

SEVENTH ORDER.—These Cows yield *two litres* a day, and continue to give milk until one month and a half advanced in gestation.

EIGHTH ORDER.—These Cows yield still less, and go dry upon being got with calf.

TABLE VI........CLASS 6.

The Square-Scutcheon Cow.

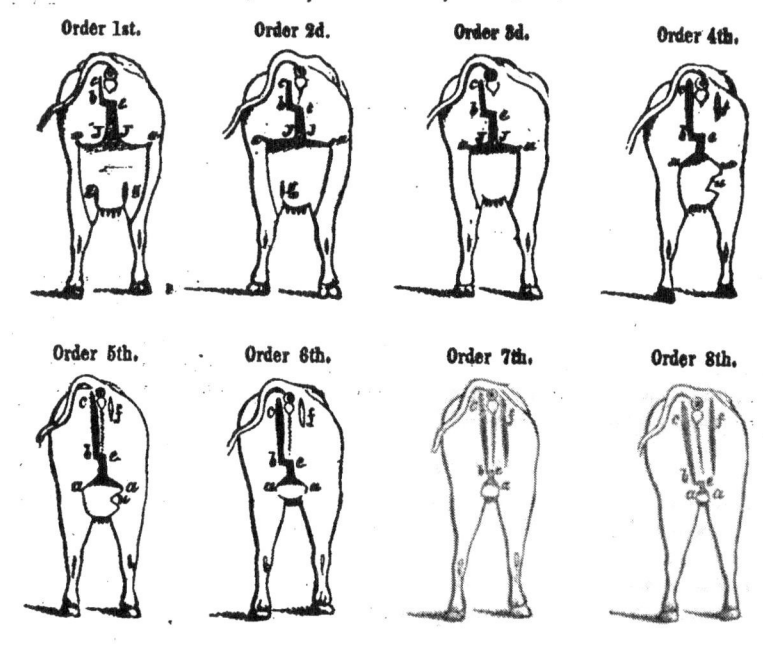

Order 1st.   Order 2d.   Order 3d.   Order 4th.

Order 5th.   Order 6th.   Order 7th.   Order 8th.

LOW COW.

FIRST ORDER.—Cows of this Order and Size yield, while at the hight of their flow, *nine litres* a day; and they continue to give milk until they are eight months gone with calf.

SECOND ORDER.—These Cows yield *eight litres* a day, and continue to give milk until seven months gone with calf.

THIRD ORDER.—These Cows yield *six litres* a day, and continue to give milk until six months gone with calf.

FOURTH ORDER.—These Cows yield *four and a half litres* a day, and continue to give milk until five months gone with calf.

FIFTH ORDER.—These Cows yield *three and a half litres* a day, and continue to give milk until four months gone with calf.

SIXTH ORDER.—These Cows yield *two and a half litres* a day, and continue to give milk until three months gone with calf.

SEVENTH ORDER.—These Cows yield *one litre* a day, and continue to give milk until a month and a half advanced in gestation.

EIGHTH ORDER.—These Cows yield still less, and go dry upon being got with calf.

BASTARD OF THE SQUARE-SCUTCHEON COW.

When the streak (O) of ascending hair on the right of the vulva consists of coarse, bristling hair, this indicates a Bastard. She will lose her milk the more promptly in proportion to the size of this growth of bristling hair, to the coarseness of the hair, and to the degree in which it bristles up and projects over; but, wherever this sign exists, the Cow will lose her milk, more or less gradually, a short time after being impregnated. The indication of this will be the more positive if the streaks above described as forming the square, to the left of the vulva, also consist of coarse, bristling hair.

CLASS VII.

The Limousine Cow.

The first Cow of this Class which came under my notice was from the Province whose name I have adopted as that of the Class. It is not to be inferred, however, that none but the Cows of Limousin belong to the Class. Its characteristic mark is to be found in all the different breeds. The name is a purely arbitrary one; and, in adopting it, I acted in the same spirit that influenced me in calling my First Class the *Flanders* Cow.

HIGH COW.

FIRST ORDER.—Cows of this Order and Size, while at the hight of their flow, yield *fourteen litres* a day, and continue to give milk until they are eight months gone with calf.

The skin, within the escutcheon formed by the growth of ascending hair, is of the same yellowish color as in the nigher Orders of the preceding Classes. The udder is delicate, and covered with short, fine, and silky hair. The growth of ascending hair begins between the teats, and on the inner side of the legs, above the hock joint, spreading outwardly, as it rises, to the points A A (see Plate VII. Order 1), on the outer surface of the thighs. From these points the escutcheon is bounded by two right lines, which run slanting downward to the points J J, which are about four inches apart. From these points two right lines rise to the point O, somewhat less than three inches below the vulva, where they meet in an acute angle.

To the right and left of the vulva are two small streaks of ascending hair (C C), about three inches or less in length, by two-fifths of an inch in width. Above the hind teats are two ovals of descending hair (G G), about four inches long, by two and a half inches in width. They are very distinguishable, by means of the whitish color of the hair within them.

These streaks, to the right and left of the vulva, do not always occur in Cows of the First Order; and they are not, therefore, to be considered as an indispensable part of the characteristic marks of this Order. The escutcheon itself, even, is sometimes imperfectly defined, and yet the Cow proves herself to be of the First Order.

SECOND ORDER.—These Cows, while at the hight of their flow, yield *twelve litres* a day, and continue to give milk until they are seven months gone with calf.

The characteristic marks are the same as in the First Order; the escutcheon, however, being on a smaller scale. The streaks (C C) to the right and left of the vulva are shorter and wider.

THIRD ORDER.—These Cows, while at the hight of their flow, yield *ten litres* a day, and continue to give milk until they are six months gone with calf.

The escutcheon is the same in shape, but more contracted. The streak (C) the vulva, to the left, is nearly five inches long, by upward of an inch in width. On the right of the vulva is a small patch of ascending hair (E), nearly three inches long, by upward of an inch in width. The point O is about six inches distant from the vulva.

FOURTH ORDER.—These Cows, while at the hight of their flow, yield *eight litres* a day, and continue to give milk until five months gone with calf.

The escutcheon is on a still smaller scale. There is but one streak (C) of ascending hair by the vulva, on the left, which is eight inches long, by something over an inch in width.

FIFTH ORDER.—These Cows, while at the hight of their flow, yield *six and a half litres* a day, and continue to give milk until they are four months gone with calf.

The escutcheon is smaller, lower down, and confined to the interior surface of the thighs. If any streaks of ascending hair occur, on the right and left of the vulva, they consist of bristling hair, and are longer and wider than in the preceding Order.

SIXTH ORDER.—These Cows, during the hight of their flow, yield *five litres* a day, and continue to give milk until they are three months gone with calf.

The escutcheon preserves its shape, but is still more contracted in its dimensions. The point O is lower down. On the left of the vulva is a streak of bristling hair, growing upward (F).

SEVENTH ORDER.—These Cows, while at the hight of their flow, yield *four litres* a day, and continue to give milk until they are one month gone with calf.

The escutcheon is smaller still. The streaks of ascending hair (F F) on the right and left of the vulva are wider, by about an inch, than those above described, and the hair is coarse and bristling.

EIGHTH ORDER.—These Cows, while at the hight of their flow, yield *two litres* a day, and go dry upon being got with calf.

The escutcheon is so small, and hid away between the thighs, as to be barely perceptible. The streaks of ascending hair (F F) are still longer and wider than in the Seventh Order.

COW OF MEDIUM HIGHT.

FIRST ORDER.—The Cows of this Order and Size, while at the hight of their flow, yield *eleven litres* a day, and continue to give milk until they are eight months gone with calf.

82 TREATISE ON MILCH COWS.

SECOND ORDER.—These Cows yield *nine litres* a day, and continue to give milk until seven months gone with calf.

THIRD ORDER.—These Cows yield *seven and a half litres* a day, and continue to give milk until six months gone with calf.

FOURTH ORDER.—These Cows yield *five and a half litres* a day, and continue to give milk until five months gone with calf.

FIFTH ORDER.—These Cows yield *four litres* a day, and continue to give milk until four months gone with calf.

SIXTH ORDER.—These Cows yield *three litres* a day, and continue to give milk until three months gone with calf.

SEVENTH ORDER.—These Cows yield *two litres* a day, and continue to give milk until two months gone with calf.

EIGHTH ORDER.—These Cows also yield *two litres* a day, and go dry upon being got with calf.

TABLE VII........CLASS 7.

The Limousine Cow.

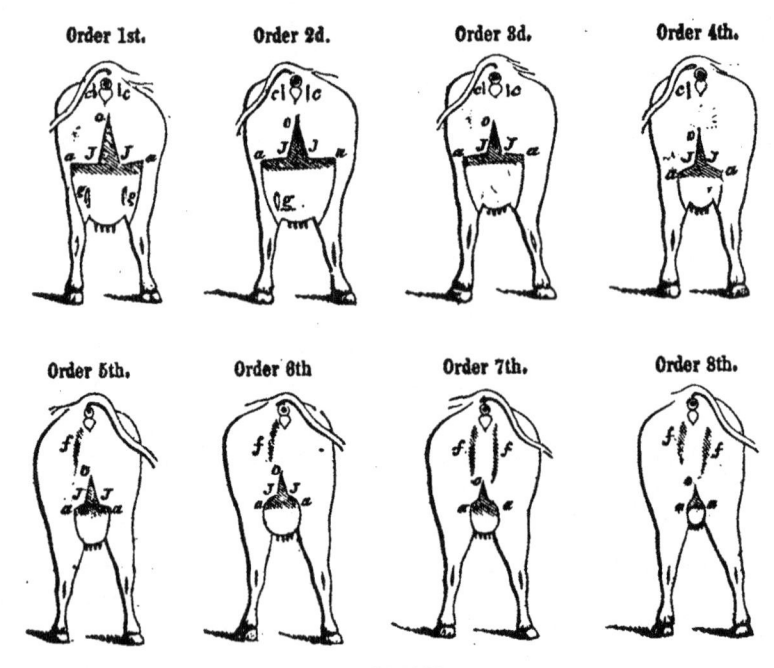

Order 1st.   Order 2d.   Order 3d.   Order 4th.

Order 5th.   Order 6th   Order 7th.   Order 8th.

LOW COW.

FIRST ORDER.—The Cows of this Order and Size yield, while at the hight of their flow, *eight litres* a day, and continue to give milk until eight months gone with calf.

SECOND ORDER.—These Cows yield *seven litres* a day, and continue to give milk until seven months gone with calf.

THIRD ORDER.—These Cows yield *six litres* a day, and continue to give milk until six months gone with calf.

FOURTH ORDER.—These Cows yield *five litres* a day, and continue to give milk until five months gone with calf.

FIFTH ORDER.—These Cows yield *four litres* a day, and continue to give milk until four months gone with calf.

SIXTH ORDER.—These Cows yield *three litres* a day, and continue to give milk until three months gone with calf.

SEVENTH ORDER.—These Cows yield *two litres* a day, and continue to give milk until one month gone with calf.

EIGHTH ORDER.—These Cows yield *one litre* a day, and go dry upon being got with calf.

BASTARD OF THE LIMOUSINE COW.

In this Class also, as in the *Curveline* and *Bicorn* Classes, the Bastard is indicated by the streaks of ascending hair (F F) to the right and left of the vulva; which streaks are of the same dimensions and of the same character generally as in those Classes. (See Plate IX. Fig. 8.)

CLASS VIII.

The Horizontal Cut Cow.

I have given this name to those Cows whose escutcheon is bounded at top by a horizontal line, which cuts the ascending hair square off just when it has spread to its greatest width. The figure (Plate VIII.) will be seen to be very different from that of the other Classes.

HIGH COW.

FIRST ORDER.—The Cows of this Order and Size, during the hight of their flow, yield *twelve litres* a day, and they continue to give milk until they are eight months gone with calf.

The skin within the escutcheon, and the dandruf from it, are of a reddish yellow. The ascending hair is short and fine; the skin beneath it quite silky; the four teats far apart. As in the other Classes, the ascending hair which forms the escutcheon begins between the four teats, and on the inner surface of the thighs, a little above the hock joint—spreading out, as it rises, to the points E E, on the outer surface of the thighs. Here it is cut short off, by a transversal or horizontal line, running across from one thigh to the other.

Although the escutcheon does not rise, as in the other Classes, to or near the vulva, we nevertheless find, on the right and left of that orifice, the two streaks of ascending hair (C C), which are so valuable, as an indication of the character of the Cow, in regard to the period during which she will continue to give milk after becoming pregnant: this point being determined by the size of these marks and the nature of the hair within them. In the present Order they consist of fine hair, and are from three and a quarter to four inches in length, by less than half an inch broad.

Above the hind teats are two little oval marks (B B), consisting of downward growing hair, distinguishable by its whitish color as well as by the direction in which it points.

SECOND ORDER.—These Cows, while at the hight of their flow, yield *ten litres* a day, and continue to give milk until they are seven months gone with calf.

The escutcheon is the same in shape as that of the First Order, but contracted in its dimensions. The streaks (C C) on the right and left of the vulva are unequal in size—the one on the left being of the same length as in the First Order, while the one on the right is considerably shorter.

In several of the Orders there is, immediately under the vulva, and touching it, a small streak of ascending hair (N), about two inches in length, by less than half an inch in breadth.

THIRD ORDER.—These Cows, while at the hight of their flow, yield *eight litres* a day, and continue to give milk until they are six months gone with calf.

The escutcheon is the same in shape, but more contracted still; the points E E are lower down and nearer together. Alongside of the vulva there is but one streak of ascending hair (G), which bristles up and projects over. This mark is from five to six inches long, by from four-fifths to six-fifths of an inch in width.

On the inner surface of the right thigh, beginning at the point A, there is a failure of the upward growing hair, which is replaced by descending hair. This downward growth of hair is wedge-shaped, pointing toward the udder; it is about eight inches long, by four inches in width. The hair is very distinguishable by its whitish color.

Although I have taken this place to make it known, this mark does not always occur in Cows of this Order, nor is it peculiar to those of the present Class.—Whenever it is found, let the Cow be of whatever Class or Order she may, it indicates that her daily yield of milk will fall about one-third short of the quantity set down as proper to a Cow of that Class and Order.

FOURTH ORDER.—These Cows, while at the hight of their flow, yield *six litres* a day, and continue to give milk until they are four and a half months gone with calf.

The escutcheon is smaller and lower down than in the Third Order. There is but one streak (N) of upward growing hair, which is betwixt the thighs, in a line with the vulva, and about two or two and a half inches from it. It is about four inches long, by four-fifths of an inch in breadth. Within the escutcheon there are two failures (A A) of the upward growing hair, like the one above described—that on the right being larger than the other.

FIFTH ORDER.—These Cows, while at the hight of their flow, yield *five litres* a day, and continue to give milk until they are three and a half months gone with calf.

The escutcheon is smaller still, and lower down. On the left of the vulva there is a streak (F) of upward growing hair, coarse and bristling. This mark is about six inches long, by an inch and a half in width.

It is to be observed, in regard to the streaks alongside of the vulva, that when they occur in a Cow of an inferior Order, such as they are described to be in the Cow of the First Order; in this case, whatever may be the inferiority of the Cow as to the quantity of her daily yield, she will continue to give her milk just as a Cow of the First Order would. That is to say, she will be just as long in going dry, after being got with calf, as a Cow of the First Order.

SIXTH ORDER.—These Cows, while at the hight of their flow, yield *four litres* a day, and continue to give milk until they are two months gone with calf.

The escutcheon is smaller, lower down, and confined to the inner surface of the thighs. The longer and broader the streaks of ascending hair (F F) on the right and left of the vulva, and the coarser and more bristling the hair, the worse the Cow will prove in regard to the time she will continue to give milk after being got with calf.

SEVENTH ORDER.—These Cows, while at the hight of their flow, yield *three litres* a day, and continue to give milk until one month gone with calf.

The escutcheon is still smaller than the last. The signs (F) of early drying up are the same as in the foregoing Order.

EIGHTH ORDER.—These Cows yield, during the hight of their flow, *two litres* a day, and go dry upon being got with calf.

The escutcheon is so hid away between the thighs as to be barely perceptible. Some coarse bristling hairs (F), which grow awry, are seen pointing toward the vulva.

TABLE VIII........CLASS 8.

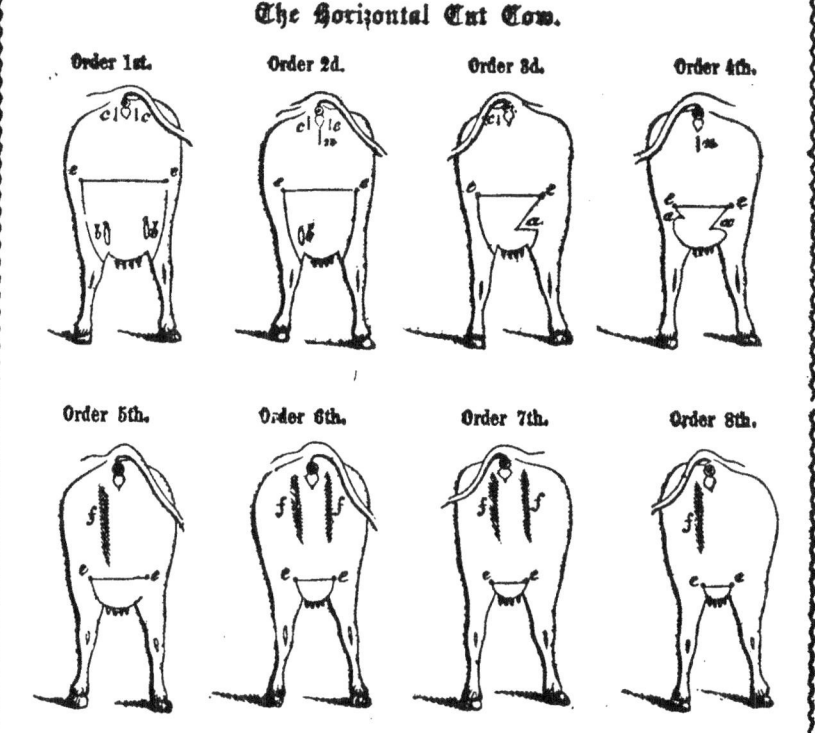

The Horizontal Cut Cow.

COW OF MEDIUM HIGHT.

FIRST ORDER.—These Cows yield, while at the hight of their flow, *nine litres* a day, and continue to give milk until they are eight months gone with calf.

SECOND ORDER.—These Cows yield *eight litres* a day, and continue to give milk until seven months gone with calf.

THIRD ORDER.—These Cows yield *seven litres* a day, and continue to give milk until five months gone with calf.

FOURTH ORDER.—These Cows yield *six litres* a day, and continue to give milk until four months gone with calf.

FIFTH ORDER.—These Cows yield *five litres* a day, and continue to give milk until three months gone with calf.

SIXTH ORDER.—These Cows yield *four litres* a day, and continue to give milk until two months gone with calf.

SEVENTH ORDER.—These Cows yield *three litres* a day, and continue to give milk until one month gone with calf.

EIGHTH ORDER.—These Cows yield *two litres* a day, and cease to give milk upon being got with calf.

LOW COW.

FIRST ORDER.—The Cows of this Order and Size, while at the hight of their flow, yield *six litres* a day, and continue to give milk until they are eight months gone with calf.

SECOND ORDER.—These Cows yield *five litres* a day, and continue to give milk until seven months gone with calf.

THIRD ORDER.—These Cows yield *four litres* a day, and continue to give milk until five months gone with calf.

FOURTH ORDER.—These Cows yield *three litres* a day, and continue to give milk until four months gone with calf.

FIFTH ORDER.—These Cows yield *two litres* a day, and continue to give milk until three months gone with calf.

SIXTH ORDER.—These Cows yield *one litre* a day, and continue to give milk until two months gone with calf.

SEVENTH AND EIGHTH ORDERS.—These Cows yield still less, and go dry upon being got with calf.

BASTARD OF THE HORIZONTAL CUT COW.

The Bastards of this Class have no escutcheon whatever. The entire space from the vulva to the udder, and on the inner surface of the thighs, is covered with hair growing downward; no growth of ascending hair is to be found upon the parts where the escutcheon occurs in the other Classes, and in the Genuine Cow of this Class.

Some of these Bastards are excellent milkers, so long as they are not impregnated; but so soon as they are got with calf, or a very short time afterward, they go dry. Those in whom the hair on the inner surface of the thighs is thick and very fine, will be found to give good rich milk. The reverse holds in regard to the quality of the milk yielded by those in whom these parts are covered with a scanty growth of coarse hair.

BASTARD BULLS.

Having attached to the portion of the work appropriated to each Class a description of the Bastard Cow belonging to it, I must indicate here the signs by which a Bastard Bull is to be known.

Bulls have escutcheons of the same shapes as those of the Cows, only, as I have already said, on a smaller scale. The growth of ascending hair which forms the escutcheon extends from the testicles upward, spreading on the inner side of the thighs. Now, whenever streaks of descending hair occur in this field of ascending hair, giving rise to lines of bristling hairs, this is to be looked upon as an indication of imperfection or bastardy; and the indication will be certain, in proportion to the size and extent of these blemishes in the escutcheon. Those Bulls in which they do not occur, and whose escutcheons, at the same time that they are free from these streaks, ascend high up, and are well developed and defined; every such Bull is to be deemed genuine, and may be relied upon for the reproduction of animals of the highest order.

TABLE IX.

The Bastard Cow of the several Classes.

1st Class. Bastard Flanders Cow. **1st Class.** Bastard Flanders Cow. **2d Class.** Bastard Selvage Cow. **3d Class.** Bastard Curveline Cow.

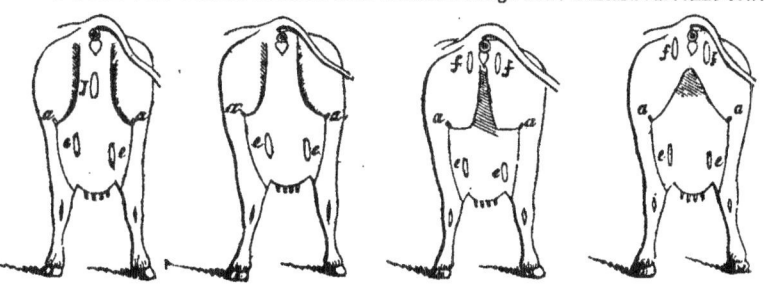

4th Class. Bastard Bicorn Cow. **5th Class.** Bastard Demijohn Cow. **6th Class.** Bast'd Sq. Scutch. Cow. **7th Class.** Bast. Limousine Cow.

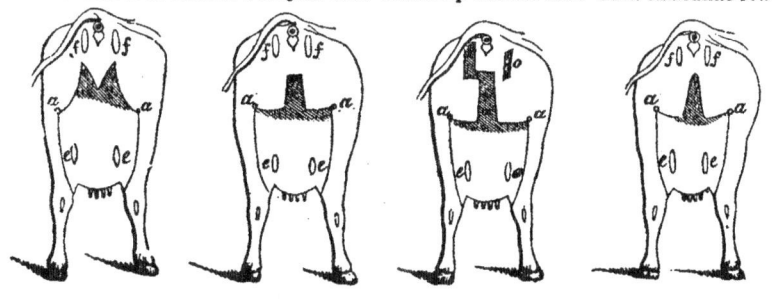

TABLE

SHOWING THE YIELD OF THE SEVERAL ORDERS OF EACH CLASS.

Class.	Order	I.	II.	III.	IV.	V.	VI.	VII.	VIII.	Litres.	Qrts.	Gills.
1. Flanders Cow.												
	High	20	18	16	14	12	9	6	4	20	21	2
	Medium	16	14	12	10	8	5	3	2			
	Low	12	10	8	6	4	3	2	1	18	19	1
2. Selvage Cow.												
	High	18	16	14	12	10	8	6	4	16	17	0
	Medium	14	13	11	10	8	6	4	3			
	Low	10	8	6	4	3	2	2	1	15	15	7½
3. Curveline Cow.												
	High	18	16	14	12	10	7	5	3	14	14	7
	Medium	18	13	11	9	7	5½	3½	2			
	Low	12	10	8	6	5	4	3	2	13	13	6½
4. Bicorn Cow.												
	High	16	14	12	10	8	6	4	3	12	12	6
	Medium	14	12	10	8	6	4	3	2½			
	Low	11	9	7	5	4	3	2	1½	11	11	5½
5. Demijohn Cow.												
	High	16	14	12	10	8	6	4	2	10	10	3
	Medium	14	12	10	8	6	5	3	2			
	Low	10	8	6½	5	4	3	2	1	9	9	4½
6. Square-Scutcheon Cow.												
	High	16	14	12	10	8	6	4	2	8	8	4
	Medium	12	10	8	6	4½	3½	2	1½			
	Low	9	8	6	4½	3½	2½	1	½	7	7	3½
7. Limousine Cow.												
	High	14	12	10	8	6½	5	4	2	6	6	3
	Medium	11	9	7½	5½	4	3	2	2			
	Low	8	7	6	5	4	3	2	1	5	5	2½
8. Horizontal Cut Cow.												
	High	12	10	8	6	5	4	3	2	4	4	2
	Medium	9	8	7	6	5	4	3	2			
	Low	6	5	4	3	2	1	less than	1	3	3	1½

SKELETON OF THE OX.

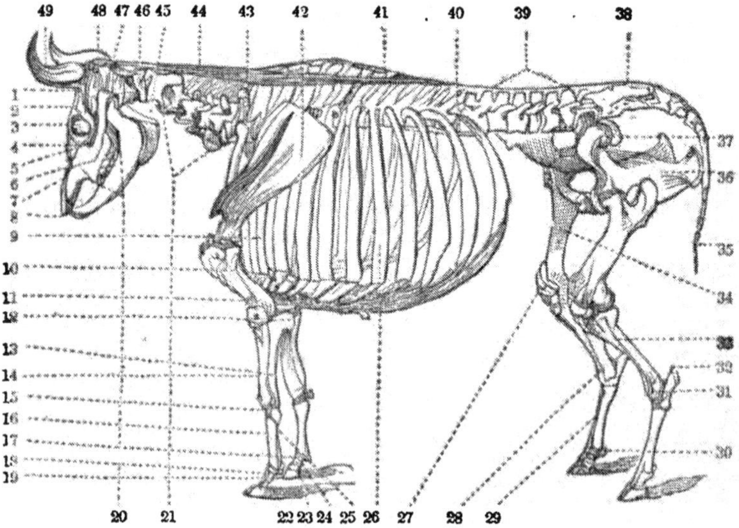

1. The temporal bone.
2. The frontal bone, or bone of the forehead.
3. The orbit of the eye.
4. The lachrymal bone.
5. The malar, or cheek bone.
6. The upper jaw-bone.
7. The nasal bone, or bone of the nose.
8. The nippers, found on the lower jaw alone.
9. The eight true ribs.
10. The humerus, or lower bone of the shoulder.
11. The sternum.
12. The ulna, its upper part forming the elbow.
13. The ulna.
14. The radius, or principal bone of the arm.
15. The small bones of the knee.
16. The large metacarpal, or shank bone.
17. The bifurcation at the pasterns, and the two larger pasterns to each foot.
18. The sessamoid bones.
19. The bifurcation of the pasterns.
20. The lower jaw and the grinders.
21. The vertebræ, or bones of the neck.
22. The navicular bones.
23. The two-coffin bones to each foot.
24. The two smaller pasterns to each foot.
25. The smaller or splint-bone.
26. The false ribs, with their cartilages.
27. The patella, or bone of the knee.
28. The small bones of the hock.
29. The metatarsals, or larger bones of the hind leg.
30. The pasterns and feet.
31. The small bones of the hock.
32. The point of the hock.
33. The tibia, or proper leg-bone.
34. The thigh-bone.
35. The bones of the tail.
36. } The haunch and pelvis.
37. }
38. The sacrum.
39. The bones of the loins.
40. The bones of the back.
41. The ligament of the neck and its attachments.
42. The scapula, or shoulder-blade.
43. The bones of the back.
44. The ligament of the neck.
45. The dentata.
46. The atlas.
47. The occipital bone, deeply depressed below the crest, or ridge of the head.
48. The parietal bone, low in the temporal fossa.
49. The horns, being processes or continuations of the frontal bone.

DICKENS'
"HOUSEHOLD WORDS:"
A NEW MONTHLY MAGAZINE,
CONDUCTED BY CHARLES DICKENS.

A Periodical with 500,000 Interested Readers.

The best investment yet—20,000 valuable ideas and delightful fancies for the trifling sum of $2!

This work combines at once the most useful instruction, the most pleasant entertainment, and is, withal, a model of style in English composition—bringing a treasure to every library, and adding a charm to every home.

Two volumes a year, containing over 1200 royal octavo pages. Terms, $2 a year, payable in advance, or 20 cents a number.

Complete sets of *Household Words* (seven volumes), and cases for uniform binding, constantly on hand.

Address all orders to

McELRATH & BARKER, Publishers, 17 Spruce st., New York.

OPINIONS OF THE PRESS;
OR A FEW WORDS FROM THOSE WHO KNOW.

"Most readers are aware that this is the title of a journal conducted by Charles Dickens. Nothing in the periodical literature of the English language gives pleasanter reading or more that is really readable in the pamplet form for the same money."—*New York Independent.*

"Abounding in pleasant and profitable reading,—an admirable family book."—*N. Y. Observer.*

"The merit of this periodical is well known. The contents are entirely original, and furnish a large amount of useful information, in a most interesting form, and at a very low price."—*Christian Advocate and Journal.*

"As a vehicle of practical knowledge, of every-day life, of sound views, and useful information, we deem it superior to any other journal or magazine. Every article is valuable and interesting."—*Religious Herald, Richmond, Va.*

"It will be difficult to find a greater variety of instructive and amusing reading."—*N. Y. Tribune.*

"This is a captivating magazine."—*N. Y. Daily Times.*

"It abounds with useful and interesting information."—*National Democrat.*

"Always welcome is this cheerful friend—always pleasing, always instructive."—*N. Y. Eve. Mirror.*

"The best of all the popular matter-of-fact periodicals."—*Literary World.*

"The most popular periodical now published, and well deserves its reputation."—*Pittsburgh Saturday Visitor.*

"It is emphatically 'Household Words,' and affords a source of amusement which no other paper can supply."—*Toledo Blade.*

"The 'Household Words' is a treasure in a family, mixing the useful with the sweet, with unrivalled skill."—*Daily (Louisville) Courier.*

"It is as pleasant and instructive as ever."—*Salem Bugle.*

"It is filled with instructive and well written articles, and it cannot have a greater circulation than it deserves. Book after book has been made up from its columns. There is not an uninteresting article in the whole work, so far as we have read."—*Louisville (Ky.) Journal.*

"The more it is read, the more it is admired."—*Aurora.*

"Its character is too well known to need any recommendation from us. Every number contains something to amuse and instruct, and the contents are always of a varied and interesting character."—*Bay State.*

"It has contained many of the choicest articles in the world of letters, and its pages are always interesting."—*Northern Democrat.*

"For originality, variety, and valuable information, it ranks high, and should be read in every home circle."—*Hartford Courier.*

"Independent of the literary beauty of some of the articles contained in the 'Household Words,' they are replete with really useful and solid information, suited to every capacity."—*Irish American.*

"Perhaps there is none which contributes more bountifully to the literary department of our popular newspapers, or has thus won a wider or better reputation beyond the limits of its own circulation."—*Penn. Freeman, Phila, Pa.*

"This magazine is a regular visitor upon our table, and we prize it more highly than any work of like character in the country. Every number is replete with the most useful and interesting matter, and of such a character as cannot fail to elevate the mind of both old and young and greatly improve the family circle."—*Covington (Ky.) Flag.*

"The articles in this magazine are all original, written in a chaste style, and the purity of the ideas and language is such as will strongly recommend it for family reading. Flashy stories are all excluded, and it is sought to convey instruction as well as amusement in every article published."—*N. Y. Atlas.*

"We have before us the 'Household Words,' a monthly journal conducted by Charles Dickens. It is the American edition of the truly original magazine conducted by 'Boz' in London. Its publishers furnish it in excellent style, and we wish them every success in this praiseworthy effort to give the reading public of this country so rich an intellectual repast. Get the book and read it. You will find it to be 'Household Words' without the baby talk."—*Flushing Journal.*

"It has probably done more good than any periodical ever printed for a similar period in the English language."—*Lord Brougham.*

BOOKS FOR YOUNG AND OLD.

For Reading, Reference, and Private Libraries.
FOR PROFESSIONAL MEN, FARMERS, AND MECHANICS.
FOR SCHOOL AND PUBLIC LIBRARIES.

For Sale by BANGS, BROTHER, & Co., 13 *Park Row New York.*

Lardner's Lectures on Science and Art:

Popular Lectures on Science and Art; by DIONYSIUS LARDNER, LL. D., Professor of Natural Philosophy and Astronomy in the University of London, &c., &c. This work is comprised in two elegant octavo volumes, neatly put up in strong muslin covers, and illustrated by several hundred Cuts and Engravings. Price $4.00.

In these published Lectures it will be found that the author has preserved the same simplicity and elegance of language, perspicuity of reasoning, and felicity of illustration, which rendered his oral discourses in the chief cities and towns in the United States so universally popular.

"Dr. Lardner has in these Lectures been peculiarly happy in communicating information in clear and perspicuous language, and by the aid of familiar illustrations presented his subjects in a manner both attractive and easily comprehended."—*F. Whittlesey.*

"I shall take great pleasure in communicating my official recommendation of these invaluable Lectures to every board of officers charged with the purchase of township and school-district libraries through the state. I hope they may reach, not only every town and school district of *this* state, but that they may be extensively circulated and read throughout our wide-spread country."—*Ira Mayhew, Superintendent of Public Instruction, State of Michigan.*

"I could wish that they were found in every school-library—to which their scientific accuracy and numerous moral reflections upon the wonderful works of God should be esteemed no small commendation. But they should be found too in every workshop in the land; for science and art are here exhibited in their true relations; and the working-men of our country would find here both entertainment and instruction, calculated to improve alike their intellects and their morals."—*D. M. Reese, Superintendent of Schools, New York City.*

Ewbank's Hydraulics and Mechanics:

A Descriptive and Historical Account of Hydraulic and other Machines for Raising Water, Ancient and Modern, with Observations on the various Subjects connected with the Mechanic Arts; including the Development of the Steam-Engine; Descriptions of every variety of Bellows, Piston, and Rotary Pumps; Fire-Engines, Water-Rams, Pressure-Engines, Air-Machines, Eolipiles, &c.; Remarks on Ancient Wells, Air-Beds, Cog-Wheels, Blowpipes, Bellows of various People, Magic Goblets, Steam-Idols and other Machinery of Ancient Temples: to which are added Experiments on Blowing and Spouting Tubes, and other original devices; Nature's Modes and Machinery for raising Water; Historical Notices respecting Siphons, Fountains, Water-Organs, Clepsydræ, Pipes, Valves, Cocks, &c., &c. Illustrated by nearly 300 Cuts and Engravings. By THOMAS EWBANK, of New York, Commissioner of Patents in the United States Patent-Office. 1 vol. 8vo. Price $2.50.

The price of the first edition of this elegant octavo was $4.50 per copy. The increased and continued sale of the work enabled the publishers to reduce the price so as to bring it within the reach of all classes.

"This is a highly valuable production, replete with novelty and interest, and adapted to gratify equally the historian, the philosopher, and the mechanician. Mr. EWBANK's work can not be too widely circulated. It is an elegant 'table-book,' suitable to all persons. Hundreds of impressive biographical and historical anecdotes, generally unknown, might be quoted as proofs of the multifarious intelligence which Mr. Ewbank has amassed for the edification of those who may study his richly-entertaining volume. We know not a compilation specifically designed to exhibit that mechanical philosophy which appertains to common, domestic, and social life, with the public weal, to which the attention of youth can be directed with equal amusement and beneficial illumination as to Mr. Ewbank's acceptable disquisitions. Therefore we earnestly recommend his volume to their study in preference to the perusal of those fantastic and pernicious fictions which pervert the imagination, and deteriorate the mind, and corrupt the morals of the thoughtless myriads who 'feed on those ashes.'"—*National Intelligencer.*

EXAMINE THESE BOOKS.

HISTORICAL WORKS.—Octavo Editions.

The following Historical Works are printed in uniform octavo volumes, on fine paper, good type, and bound in a substantial manner. In ordering any of these works, to insure the genuine edition, it will be well always to designate the *octavo* edition.

The Hon. DANIEL WEBSTER, in his "Discourse before the New York Historical Society," speaking of the authors of these histories, says:—

"Our great teachers and examples in the historical art are, doubtless, the eminent historians of the Greek and Roman ages. In their several ways, they are the masters to whom all succeeding times have looked for instruction and improvement. They are the models which have stood the test of time, and, like the glorious creations in marble of Grecian genius, have been always admired and never surpassed."

Herodotus's Ancient History:

The Ancient History of Herodotus; translated from the original Greek, by Rev. WILLIAM BELOE; with the Life of Herodotus, by LEONARD SCHMITZ, LL. D., F. R. S. E., &c., &c. 1 vol. 8vo—strong cloth.—Price $2.00.

"We have our favorites in literature, as well as other things, and, 1 confess, that, among the Grecian writers, my estimate of Herodotus is great. His evident truthfulness, his singular simplicity of style, and his constant respect and veneration for sacred and divine things, win my regard. It is true that he sometimes appears credulous, which caused Aristotle to say of him, that he was a story-teller. But, in respect to this, two things are to be remarked; the one is, that he never avers as a fact that which rests on the accounts of others; the other is, that all subsequent travels and discoveries have tended to confirm his fidelity. From his great qualities as a writer, as well as from the age in which he lived, he is justly denominated the "Father of History." Herodotus was a conscientious narrator of what he saw and heard. In his manner there is much of the old epic style; indeed, his work may be considered as the connecting link between the epic legend and political history; truthful, on the one hand, since it was a genuine history; but, on the other, conceived and executed in the spirit of poetry, and not the profounder spirit of political philosophy. It breathes a reverential submission to the Divine will, and recognises distinctly the governing hand of Providence in the affairs of men. * * He travelled to collect the materials for his History—he made of them one whole, and laid one idea at the bottom, with as much epic simplicity as Homer did in the Iliad."—*Daniel Webster.*

"Herodotus is styled the 'Father of History,' because he was the first who wrote general history, and the first to adorn it with the graces of eloquence. So delightful and engaging is he in narrative, and such perfect simplicity is there in his manner, that we fancy we see before our eyes a venerable old man, just returned from his travels through distant countries, and, sitting down in his arm-chair, relating without restraint all that he has seen and heard. His style seems to have been formed by his native good taste, and by practice, rather than by the rules of art; for at that period the writing of prose was not very common. The text of this edition is printed very carefully and accurately, and in every respect pains have been taken to make it the most acceptable for private and public libraries, for schools, and for the mere readers for amusement."

Thucydides:

History of the Peloponnesian War. Translated from the Greek of Thucydides, to which is prefixed a Life of Thucydides, his Qualifications as an Historian, and a Survey of the History. By WILLIAM SMITH, D.D. 1 vol. 8vo. Price $1.75.

"In Thucydides, the art of History is further advanced, though he lived very little later than Herodotus, and probably had read or heard his history, though that is doubted.

"Thucydides did not, indeed, make one whole of his work, for he did not survive the war whose history he undertook to relate; but he is less credulous than Herodotus; he has no proper dialogue; he is more compact; he indulges very little in episodes; he draws characters, and his speeches are more like formal, stately discussions. And he says of them, they are such as he either heard himself, or received from those who did hear them, and he states that he gives them in their true substance. There is nothing to create a doubt that personally he heard the oration of Pericles.

"In short, Herodotus's work seems a natural, fresh production of the soil; that of Thucydides belongs to a more advanced state of culture. Quinctilian says of the former, *In Herodoto omnia leniter fluunt,* of the latter, *Densus et brevis et semper instans sibi.*

"But, upon the whole, I am compelled to regard Thucydides as the greater writer. Thucydides was equally truthful, but more conversant with the motives and character of men in their political relations. He took infinite pains to make himself thoroughly acquainted with transactions that occurred in his own day, and which became the subject of his own narrative.

"It is said, even, that persons were employed by him to obtain information from both the belligerent powers, for his use, while writing the history of the Peloponnesian war.

"He was one of the most eminent citizens of the Athenian Republic, educated under the institutions of Solon, and trained in all the political wisdom, these institutions had developed, in the two centuries since their establishment. A more profound intellect never applied itself to historical investigation; a more clear-sighted and impartial judge of human conduct, never dealt with the fortunes and acts of political communities.

"The work of Herodotus is graphic, fluent, dramatic, and ethical in the highest degree; but it is not the work of a free citizen of a free republic, personally experienced in the conduct of its affairs. The history of the Peloponnesian war, on the other hand, could only have been produced by a man who added to vast genius deep personal insight into the workings of various public institutions.

"As Thucydides himself says, his history was written not for the entertainment of the moment, but to be 'a possession for ever.'"—*Daniel Webster.*

"Thucydides possessed peculiar qualifications for the office of historian of the Peloponnesian war, as he was a man of thorough cultivation, and an actor in the scenes which he depicts; he devoted twenty-seven years to the production of this work, which he said should be 'an eternal possession.' His style is concise, vigorous, and significant, and his history evinces the most conscientious regard for truth and justice. His work stands alone, and, in its kind, has neither equal nor rival. His pictures are frequently striking and tragic, from his severe simplicity and minute particularity, as in the description of the plague at Athens, and in the incomparable account of the Athenian expedition into Sicily and its melancholy termination. The translation of Dr Smith is admitted by judicious critics to be decidedly the best, in artistic execution and in those qualities desirable in such a performance, that has been made."

Cæsar and Sallust:

The Commentaries of Cæsar. Translated into English, to which is prefixed a Discourse concerning the Roman Art of War, by WILLIAM DUNCAN; and a Life of Cæsar by LEONARD SCHMITZ, LL.D., F.R.S.C., &c., &c.

The History of the Conspiracy of Catiline, and the Jugurthine War. By C. CRISPUS SALLUSTIUS. Translated by WILLIAM ROSE.

These two works are bound together in one neat octavo volume. Price $1.75.

"Cæsar, one of the most distinguished of all great men, wrote accounts of what he had done, or what related directly to himself. The clearness, purity and precision of his style are as characteristic of him as any of his great achievements."—*Daniel Webster.*

"Of the Roman writers, my preference is strongly for Sallust. I admire his reach of thought, his clearness of style, as well as his accuracy of narration. He is sufficiently concise; he is sententious without being meager or obscure, and his power of personal and individual description is remarkable. There are, indeed, in his style, some roughnesses belonging to the Roman tongue at an earlier age, but they seem to strengthen the structure of his sentences, without especially injuring their beauty. No character drawing can well exceed his delineation of Catiline, his account of Jugurtha, or his parallel between Cæsar and Cato. I have thought, sometimes, that I saw resemblances between his terse and powerful periods, and the remarks and sayings of Dr. Johnson, as they appear, not in his stately performances, but in the record of his conversations, by Boswell."—*Daniel Webster.*

"All possible care has been taken to render this edition of Cæsar's Commentaries exact, and to preserve the distinctness and perspicuity of expression for which the original is so justly famous. The discourse concerning the military customs of the ancient Romans contains much that is curious and most interesting in relation to the art of War. Besides the seven books of the Gallic War, and the three of the Civil, written by Cæsar himself, the Supplements of A. Hirtius Pansa are inserted, consisting of an additional book to the Gallic War, and three books of the Alexandrian, African, and Spanish Wars; with an Ancient and Modern Geographical Index; to which is appended Sallust's History of the Conspiracy of Catiline and the Jugurthine War. The Life of Cæsar, by Professor Schmitz, is a valuable addition to the work."

Baker's Livy:

The History of Rome. By TITUS LIVIUS. Translated from the original, with Notes and Illustrations. By GEORGE BAKER. 2 volumes 8vo. Price $4.00.

"There is an epic completeness in his [Livy's] great work. His style is rich and flowing; his descriptions excellent; and, indeed, there is a nobleness and grandeur about his whole work, well fitted to his magnificent purpose in writing it."—*Daniel Webster.*

"There are many reasons for regarding Livy as the greatest of the ancient historians. His style may be pronounced almost faultless; and a great proof of its excellence is, that the charms with which it is invested are so little salient and so equally diffused, that all the parts in their proportion seem to unite to produce a form of the rarest beauty and grace. The charms of his manner and spirit, the truth of his statements, and the justness of his views, will for ever preserve his work among the most delightful and most valuable products of genius and intellectual toil. The translation by Baker is decidedly the best ever made into English. It preserves much of the tone, and is singularly faithful to the sense, of the illustrious Roman. The notes, and other illustrations which are added, embrace whatever useful learning has been contributed by scholars for the best appreciation of the author and his subject."

EXAMINE THESE BOOKS.

Thaër's Agriculture:

The Principles of Agriculture, by ALBERT D. THAER; translated by William Shaw and Cuthbert W. Johnson, Esq., F. R. S. With a Memoir of the Author. 1 vol. 8vo—strong cloth. Price $2.00.

This work is regarded by those who are competent to judge, as one of the most beautiful works that has ever appeared on the subject of agriculture. At the same time that it is eminently practical, it is philosophical, and, even to the general reader, remarkably entertaining.

Von THAER was educated for a physician; and, after reaching the summit of his profession, he retired into the country, where his garden soon became the admiration of the citizens: and when he began to lay out plantations and orcnards, to cultivate herbage and vegetables, the whole country was astonished at his science in the art of cultivation. He soon entered upon a large farm, and opened a school for the study of Agriculture, where his fame became known from one end of Europe to the other.

This great work of Von Thaer's has passed through four editions in the United States, but it is still comparatively unknown. The attention of owners of landed estates in cities and towns, as well as those persons engaged in the practical pursuits of agriculture, is earnestly requested to this volume.

Randall's Sheep-Husbandry:

Sheep-Husbandry; with an Account of the different Breeds, and General Directions in regard to Summer and Winter Management, Breeding, and the Treatment of Diseases. With numerous Portraits and Engravings of Sheep, Shepherds, Dogs, &c. By HENRY S. RANDALL, Secretary of State of the State of New York. 1 vol. 8vo—strong cloth. Price $1.50.

"This is probably the most elaborate, original, and useful work, which has ever appeared on the important subject of sheep-culture. The author in his introduction says that, while he has carefully reviewed and collated the opinions of other writers on doubtful practical points, he has in all instances preferred the results of his own personal experience and observation. The English and German systems of management he regards as almost wholly inapplicable here, on account of the different relation which the prices of land and labor bear toward each other in those countries and our own.

"This work is earnestly recommended to all owners or tillers of land, as affording such valuable information as may greatly increase the value of their lands or the products of labor."

Arago's Astronomy:

Popular Lectures on Astronomy, by M. ARAGO. With Additions and Corrections, by Doctor LARDNER. Containing numerous Illustrations. Fifth Edition. 96 pp. 8vo. Price 25 cents.

"To all who are conversant with the existing state of astronomical science in Europe, it is well known that, in addition to the regular duties of his office as royal astronomer of France, M. Arago has been in the practice of delivering, each season, at the 'Observatoire,' a course of lectures of a popular kind, which are attended by all classes of well-informed persons, including ladies in considerable numbers. These discourses are given extemporaneously in the strictest sense of the term, and in style and character bear a close analogy to those delivered by Dr. Lardner in this country within the last few years. It does not appear that M. Arago ever designed their publication, nor that he ever even committed them to writing. A person employed by one of the Brussels publishers reported them; and the publication, reputed to be M. Arago's lectures, is nothing more than this report, which, though it could not be legally published or circulated in France, obtained through the Belgian booksellers and their correspondents an extensive illegal circulation in that country. A translation of this report was circulated largely in England."

The publishers of the present volume, being aware that errors of a more or less important kind must, under such circumstances, have prevailed in the original Belgian edition, and still more in the English translation, and that omissions and chasms must have required to be filled up by some person conversant with the science, and capable of writing upon it in a clear and familiar style, applied to Dr. Lardner, and induced him to revise the reported lectures, and to add to them such topics as might appear desirable to give them increased utility. The result of this arrangement has been the present volume.

The Zion Songster:

The Zion Songster: a Collection of Hymns and Spiritual Songs, generally sung at Camp and Prayer Meetings, and in Revivals of Religion. Neatly bound in roan, with stamped sides, and sold at 30 cents per copy retail. Over fifty thousand copies of this little Work have been sold.

EXAMINE THESE BOOKS.

Shelley's Poetical Works (complete):

The Poetical Works of PERCY BYSSHE SHELLEY. With Remarks on the Poetical Faculty, and its Influence on Human Destiny, embracing a Biographical and Critical Notice, by G. G. FOSTER. 1 vol. 12mo, 750 pp. Price $1.50.

This is by far the fullest and most complete edition of Shelley's works which has appeared. The favor with which it has been received may be inferred from the fact that three large editions have been called for, and are already sold. This edition contains all the accredited poetical works of Shelley, with his own notes and those of his wife.

"No modern poet," says R. H. Stoddard, "was ever so chivalrous and lofty in his sentiments and actions."—"He was a greater man than his noble friend Byron," continues the same writer, "for he never complained. In every page of his writings, Hope and Faith go hand in hand. No man, excepting Shakspere, ever wrote so much, and so well. Everything in his poetry seems to set itself to the finest music. He is every day becoming more popular, and thousands who know nothing of poetry appreciate and love the intense beauty and hope of this great and noble-hearted poet."

German Phrase-Book:

A Phrase-Book in English and German, with a Literal Translation of the German into English, arranged on the Plan of a Dictionary; together with a Complete Explanation of the Sounds and the Accentuation of the German. By MORITZ ERTHEILER. Fifth Edition. 1 vol. 18mo, 172 pages. Price, in paper covers, 25 cents.

This is a very useful little work for persons who are learning the German language.

"I take the greatest pleasure in recommending Mr. Ertheiler's 'Phrase-Book' to both teachers and learners of the German language."—C. J. HEMPEL, M. D.

"I avow with great frankness that it is the best little work of the kind I am acquainted with."—F. J. GRUND.

"It seems to me to be admirably fitted to enable the student to obtain in the shortest period possible an accurate as well as a ready acquaintance with the German language."—H. VETHAKE.

History of Shoes and Shoemakers:

The Book of the Feet: a History of Boots and Shoes, with Illustrations of the Fashions of the Egyptians, Hebrews, Persians, Greeks, and Romans, and the prevailing Styles throughout Europe during the Middle Ages, down to the Present Period. Also, Hints to Lastmakers, and Remedies for Corns, &c. By J. SPARKES HALL, Patent Elastic Bootmaker to her Majesty the Queen, the Queen Dowager, &c. With a History of Boots and Shoes in the United States, Biographical Sketches of eminent Shoemakers, and Crispin Anecdotes. Price 50 cents. A book addressed to those who wear Boots and Shoes, and also to those who make them.

"Mr. Hall is the most fashionable among the London bootmakers; and his book has been received with decided favor in the higher circles."—*London Times.*

... "For such visions as these, the disciples of the lapstone should be grateful.... The sons of Crispin, and every man who has a soul should reward the publishers' enterprise in the preparation of this elegant volume."—*Literary World.*

"Every lady who wishes a neat foot and a good fit, should carry this book with her to her shoemaker.... To persons engaged in the boot and shoe trade, this work will prove of great value, while to the general reader it will be found more than usually interesting."—*Home Journal.*

"A complete revolution is likely to be made in the style of manufacturing shoes, in consequence of the publication of the 'Book of the Feet.' Ladies about ordering their summer-boots would do well to consult this work before calling on their shoemaker."—*Tribune.*

Life of Henry Clay: (In Press.)

The Life of Henry Clay; from his Birth, brought down to the Present Time. By EPES SARGENT, Esq. 1 vol. 8vo, in cloth binding. Price 75 cents.

This edition of the Life of Mr. CLAY will be the most full and accurate of any which has ever appeared.

The above Books may be procured from any of the Booksellers, or orders may be sent to BANGS, BROTHER, & CO., 13 *Park Row, New York.*

EXAMINE THESE BOOKS.

Baines's Wars of the French Revolution:

History of the Wars of the French Revolution, from the breaking out of the War in 1792 to the Restoration of a General Peace in 1815; comprehending the Civil History of Great Britain and France during that period. By EDWARD BAINES. With an Original History of the Last War between the United States and Great Britain, by WILLIAM GRIMSHAW, of Philadelphia. 2 vols. 8vo—strong cloth. Price $4.00.

This history of the wars of Europe during the eventful period embraced within its pages has passed through several large editions in this country, but the high price at which it was sold has heretofore tended to limit its circulation. The present edition is sold at a price which will enable almost every family and library to possess themselves of one of the most interesting historical records which were ever printed.

"It is a clear, impartial narrative; succinct, without injurious brevity, and dispassionate without descending to unanimated tameness. As a history of the events which it professes peculiarly to treat, it has no superior, and may justly be characterized as one of the most valuable records that ever issued from the press."

Ferguson's Rome:

History of the Progress and Termination of the Roman Republic, by ADAM FERGUSON. With a Notice of the Author, by Lord JEFFREY. 1 vol., 8vo. Price $1.75.

"This work has been translated into several modern languages, and has been justly described as one which not only delights by the clearness of its narrative and the boldness of its descriptions, but instructs and animates by profound and masterly delineations of character, as well as by the philosophical precision with which it traces the connection of events. It is written in that tone of highminded enthusiasm which, if it can only snatch from oblivion whatever is noble and generous in the record of human actions, regards the graces of style as objects merely of secondary account, and is chiefly studious of impressing the lessons of wisdom which may be gathered from the survey of distant ages."

Gillies' Greece:

The History of Ancient Greece, its Colonies and Conquests, to the Division of the Macedonian Empire; including the History of Literature, Philosophy, and Fine Arts. By JOHN GILLIES, LL. D., F. A. S. 1 vol. 8vo—strong cloth. Price $2.00.

"The best critics have regarded this History of Greece by the royal historiographer of the University of Glasgow as one of the masterpieces of historical literature in our language. This edition is from that which received the author's last corrections and improvements."

The Tatler and Guardian:

The Tatler and Guardian, chiefly by Sir RICHARD STEELE and JOSEPH ADDISON; and an Account of the Authors, by THOMAS BABBINGTON MACAULAY. With Notes and Indexes. 1 vol. 8vo—neatly bound in cloth. Price $2.50.

"In the prose literature of the English language it will be admitted, by all thoroughly-educated critics, that there is nothing upon the whole more admirable than those splendid series of papers by ADDISON, STEELE, and their associates, commencing with 'The Tatler,' and ending with 'The Guardian.' In morals and sentiment there is nothing more just and manly, and in style they are still the unapproachable models by which all the highest achievements in this department of authorship are judged. They are worthy to be ranked with the immortal poems which in a previous age were produced by Shakspere, Spenser, and Milton. If any man of our own generation is entitled to sit in judgment upon the works of the great English essayists of Queen Anne's time, that man is Thomas Babbington Macaulay, whose criticism is prefixed to this edition."

POPULAR LECTURES ON
ASTRONOMY,
BY M. ARAGO;
WITH ADDITIONS AND CORRECTIONS,
BY DR. LARDNER:

ILLUSTRATED BY FIFTY-THREE DIAGRAMS OR ENGRAVINGS.

PUBLISHERS' PREFACE.

To all who are conversant with the existing state of Astronomical Science in Europe, it is well known that, in addition to the regular duties of his office as Royal Astronomer of France, M. Arago has been in the practice of delivering each season, at the *Observatoire*, a Course of Lectures of a popular kind, which are attended by all classes of well-informed persons, including ladies in considerable numbers. These discourses are given extemporaneously in the strictest sense of the term, and in style and character bear a close analogy to those delivered by Dr. Lardner in this country within the last few years. It does not appear that M. Arago ever designed their publication, nor that he ever even committed them to writing. A person employed by one of the Brussels publishers reported them, and the publication reputed to be M. Arago's Lectures is nothing more than this report, which though it could not be legally published or circulated in France, obtained through the Belgian booksellers and their correspondents an extensive illegal circulation in that country. A translation of this report was circulated largely in England.

The publishers of the present volume, being aware that errors of a more or less important kind must, under such circumstances, have prevailed in the original Belgian edition, and still more in the English translation, and that omissions and chasms must have required to be filled up by some person conversant with the Science, and capable of writing upon it in an easy and familiar style, applied to Dr. Lardner, and induced him to revise the reported Lectures, and to add to them such topics as might appear desirable to give them increased utility. The result of this arrangement has been the present volume.

Dr Lardner desires it to be understood that he should not have felt himself justified in interpolating any work, however elementary, published with the actual sanction of M. Arago's name. But, it being understood, and indeed manifested by unequivocal internal evidence, that the Belgian report was unauthorized and unauthentic, and the circulation of some translation of it in this country being rendered inevitable by the very popularity of its reputed author, it was better that a carefully revised copy should be published than a mere reprint of the English translation of the imperfect Belgian report.

CONTENTS:

LECTURE I.
General Laws of the Reflection of Light—General Laws of the Refraction of Light—Lenses—Refracting and Reflecting Telescopes—Structure of the Eye.

LECTURE II.
History of Astronomy—Preliminary Ideas—Definitions—Capricornus (Caper)—Aquarius—Pisces—Aries—Taurus—Gemini—Cancer—Leo—Virgo—Libra—Scorpio—Sagittarius.

LECTURE III.
Aspect of the Heavens—Apparent Motions of the Heavenly Bodies.

LECTURE IV.
The Fixed Stars.

LECTURE V.
Distances of the Planets—The Sun—Physical Constitution of the Sun—The Moon—Physical Constitution of the Moon.

LECTURE VI.
Mercury—Physical Constitution of Mercury—Venus—Appearance of Venus as she moves round the Sun—Physical Constitution of Venus. Superior Planets: Mars—Physical Constitution of Mars—The four Telescopic Planets: Juno, Ceres, Pallas, Vesta.

LECTURE VII.
Jupiter and his Satellites—Physical Constitution of Jupiter—Saturn, his Ring and his Satellites—Herschel, or Uranus, and his Satellites.

LECTURE VIII.
Distances, Diameters, Volumes, &c. of the Planets—Kepler's Laws—Universal Attraction—Of the Masses of the Planets.

LECTURE IX.
Figure of the Earth—Dimensions of the Earth—The Earth's Motion—Diurnal Rotation of the Earth—Annual Motion of Earth.

LECTURE X.
Inequalities of the Moon and of the Earth.

LECTURE XI.
Comets—Halley's and other Comets—Physical Constitution of Comets.

LECTURE XII.
Eclipses of the Moon—Eclipses of the Sun.

LECTURE XIII.
The Tides.

LECTURE XIV.
Determination of Latitude and Longitude.

LECTURE XV.
The Atmosphere—Of the Moon in the Horizon—The Harvest Moon.

LECTURE XVI.
The Seasons and the Days—The Earth's Temperature.

LECTURE XVII.
The Calendar.

APPENDIX.
Table of the Constellations, with the Number of Stars in each, as far as those of the sixth magnitude—Summary.

☞ The above work is neatly printed, and well done up in paper covers, and sold at the low price of 25 cents.

EXAMINE THESE WORKS.

Guénon on Milch Cows:

A Treatise on Milch Cows, whereby the Quality and Quantity of Milk which any Cow will give may be accurately determined, by observing Natural Marks or External Indications alone; the length of time she will continue to give Milk, &c., &c. By M. FRANCIS GUENON, of Libourne, France. Translated by NICHOLAS P. TRIST, Esq.; with Introductory Remarks and Observations on the Cow and the Dairy, by JOHN S. SKINNER. Illustrated with numerous Engravings. Price for single copies, neatly done up in paper covers, 37½ cents; library edition, full bound in cloth, and lettered, 62½ cents. The usual discount to Booksellers, Agents, Country Merchants, and Pedlars.

This extraordinary book has excited the attention of the ablest agriculturists of the country. Five thousand copies were sold in the first four weeks of its publication in New York, since which time fourteen large editions have been disposed of. The publishers have received numerous testimonials as to the usefulness and accuracy of Guénon's theory. The practical remarks and the useful information contained in the first part of the book are worth more to any farmer than the whole cost.

Under the operation of this system, which enables every one to select and put aside for the butcher calves that will be sure to prove bad-milkers, the WHOLE RACE of milch cattle may be rapidly improved throughout the Union. The "Boston Traveller" contains an account of the proceedings of an agricultural meeting, held in the legislative hall, in Boston, from which we make the following extracts:

"Mr. Brooks made some remarks on the ability of any one to learn to distinguish the qualities of a cow by examination. He had a very high opinion of a French work, by GUENON, recently published in New York. By the aid of that work, a man might select his stock with almost infallible certainty. He believed he could tell within a few quarts what a cow would yield of milk, and within a few pounds what she would yield of butter. He had not missed in more than ten instances out of between three and four hundred trials. He had known one cow that was not dry for fourteen years, and had calves every year.

"Mr. Denny fully accorded with Mr. Brooks in his estimate of the treatise on cattle by GUENON. He had tested its value by distributing a number of copies among intelligent, practical farmers; and their united report was in favor of the high value of the work. One of them went so far as to say that a farmer keeping twenty cows could well afford to give $100 for this treatise, if it could not be obtained at a less cost.

"Mr. French expressed his entire confidence in GUENON's treatise, and thought its introduction among our farmers was destined to work an entire revolution. For some time, none of the agricultural societies of France would give any heed to his suggestions; but when, at length, one of them was induced to put him to the test, they were perfectly astonished at the accuracy with which he applied his rules for determining the milk-giving qualities of a cow."

Numerous letters from different parts of the United States fully corroborate the theory of M. Guénon. We select the following:

"DEAR SIR: I received your favor, desiring me to state my opinion of the value of M. Guénon's 'Treatise on Milch Cows,' translated from the French. . . . . I immediately commenced the study and application of his method to every cow that came under my observation. I have examined more than one hundred cows, and, after carefully marking their escutcheons, I have become satisfied that M. Guénon's discovery is one of great merit, and can be relied upon as true. I have no doubt that I can judge very nearly as to the quantity and quality of the milk any cow will give at the height of her flow, and also the time she will continue in milk after being with calf.

"The way taken to convince myself of the truth of M. Guénon's method has been to visit the cow-yards of some of our principal dairy-farmers, and examine the escutcheons and marks on their cows, and make up my judgment as to the quantity and quality of the milk each cow would give at the height of her flow, and how long she would continue in milk after being with calf; then inquire of the owners how much milk their several cows would give at the height of their flow, and how long they would hold out after being with calf; comparing the owner's account with my own judgment. I find I have mistaken in only five cases out of more than one hundred examined.

"I consider it one of the great discoveries of the age. The advantage of this discovery to our dairy-farmers, enabling them, as I think it does, to determine the milking properties of their young stock at an early age, must be very great. In my opinion, no dairy-farmer, after acquainting himself with M. Guénon's discovery, need possess himself of a bad milking-cow.

"M. Guénon informs us that his system is applicable to calves three or four months old. I have traced the escutcheons upon calves as early as two or three weeks old, and I see no reason why their value as future milkers may not be judged of at this as well as at any other age.

"Princeton, Mass." "JOHN BROOKS."

"I have read with great satisfaction M. Guénon's work on Milch Cows, by which one can judge by certain infallible signs the milking qualities of the animal. I have compared the marks he gives for his first-grade Flanders cow, and find they correspond with the escutcheon of my favorite Devon cow 'Ellen,' that has taken the first premium at two cattle-shows of the American Institute. My farmer has great faith in M. Guénon's work, and so has one of my neighbors, a knowing Scotch milkman, who keeps fifty cows. He says that, after careful examination, he places confidence in these marks, and they will govern him in his future purchases. I shall hereafter make my selection of the calves I will raise from my choice stocks from the marks given by this author. I think every farmer should own this work. "ROSWELL L. COLT, Paterson, N. J."

"Having had experience in raising cows, I was pleased to find a treatise on the subject by M. Guénon, of Libourne, in France—which I procured and carefully studied. I think the book more worthy of attention than I believe it has received. I found that his marks of the particular classes and orders of cows agree with nearly all I have had an opportunity to examine. It is easy to ascertain, after studying this book, to which class and order almost every cow belongs, which, as a guide in purchasing milch cows, or of safely deciding which to keep, before we have had time or opportunity to test their qualities as milkers, will far more than repay the price of the book, and the time necessary to a clear understanding of it. "JESSE CHARLTON, East-Windsor Hill, Conn."

DICKENS' "HOUSEHOLD WORDS:"
A NEW MONTHLY MAGAZINE,
CONDUCTED BY CHARLES DICKENS.

A Periodical with 500,000 Interested Readers.

The best investment yet—20,000 valuable ideas and delightful fancies for the trifling sum of $2!

This work combines at once the most useful instruction, the most pleasant entertainment, and is, withal, a model of style in English composition—bringing a treasure to every library, and adding a charm to every home.

Two volumes a year, containing over 1200 royal octavo pages. Terms, $2 a year, payable in advance, or 20 cents a number.

Complete sets of *Household Words* (seven volumes), and cases for uniform binding, constantly on hand.

Address all orders to

McELRATH & BARKER, Publishers, 17 Spruce st., New York.

OPINIONS OF THE PRESS;
OR A FEW WORDS FROM THOSE WHO KNOW.

"Most readers are aware that this is the title of a journal conducted by Charles Dickens. Nothing in the periodical literature of the English language gives pleasanter reading or more that is really readable in the pamflet form for the same money."—*New York Independent.*

"Abounding in pleasant and profitable reading,—an admirable family book."—*N. Y. Observer.*

"The merit of this periodical is well known. The contents are entirely original, and furnish a large amount of useful information, in a most interesting form, and at a very low price."—*Christian Advocate and Journal.*

"As a vehicle of practical knowledge, of every-day life, of sound views, and useful information, we deem it superior to any other journal or magazine. Every article is valuable and interesting."—*Religious Herald, Richmond, Va.*

"It will be difficult to find a greater variety of instructive and amusing reading."—*N. Y. Tribune.*

"This is a captivating magazine."—*N. Y. Daily Times.*

"It abounds with useful and interesting information."—*National Democrat.*

"Always welcome is this cheerful friend—always pleasing, always instructive."—*N. Y. Eve. Mirror.*

"The best of all the popular matter-of-fact periodicals."—*Literary World.*

"The most popular periodical now published, and well deserves its reputation."—*Pittsburgh Saturday Visitor.*

"It is emphatically 'Household Words,' and affords a source of amusement which no other paper can supply."—*Toledo Blade.*

"The 'Household Words' is a treasure in a family, mixing the useful with the sweet, with unrivalled skill."—*Daily (Louisville) Courier.*

"It is as pleasant and instructive as ever."—*Salem Bugle.*

"It is filled with instructive and well written articles, and it cannot have a greater circulation than it deserves. Book after book has been made up from its columns. There is not an uninteresting article in the whole work, so far as we have read."—*Louisville (Ky.) Journal.*

"The more it is read, the more it is admired."—*Aurora.*

"Its character is too well known to need any recommendation from us. Every number contains something to amuse and instruct, and the contents are always of a varied and interesting character."—*Bay State.*

"It has contained many of the choicest articles in the world of letters, and its pages are always interesting."—*Northern Democrat.*

"For originality, variety, and valuable information, it ranks high, and should be read in every home circle."—*Hartford Courier.*

"Independent of the literary beauty of some of the articles contained in the 'Household Words,' they are replete with really useful and solid information, suited to every capacity."—*Irish American.*

"Perhaps there is none which contributes more bountifully to the literary department of our popular newspapers, or has thus won a wider or better reputation beyond the limits of its own circulation."—*Penn. Freeman, Phila., Pa.*

"This magazine is a regular visitor upon our table, and we prize it more highly than any work of like character in the country. Every number is replete with the most useful and interesting matter, and of such a character as cannot fail to elevate the mind of both old and young and greatly improve the family circle."—*Covington (Ky.) Flag.*

"The articles in this magazine are all original, written in a chaste style, and the purity of the ideas and language is such as will strongly recommend it for family reading. Flashy stories are all excluded, and it is sought to convey instruction as well as amusement in every article published."—*N. Y. Atlas.*

"We have before us the 'Household Words,' a monthly journal conducted by Charles Dickens. It is the American edition of the truly original magazine conducted by 'Boz' in London. Its publishers furnish it in excellent style, and we wish them every success in this praiseworthy effort to give the reading public of this country so rich an intellectual repast. Get the book and read it. You will find it to be 'Household Words' without the baby talk."—*Flushing Journal.*

"It has probably done more good than any periodical ever printed for a similar period in the English language."—*Lord Brougham.*